Heroes of History

Benjamin Rush

The Common Good

I08772277

HEROES OF HISTORY

BENJAMIN RUSH

The Common Good

JANET & GEOFF BENGE

Emerald Books

P.O. BOX 635, LYNNWOOD, WA 98046

Emerald Books are distributed through YWAM Publishing. For a full list of titles, including other great biographies, visit our website at www.emeraldbooks.com.

Benjamin Rush: The Common Good
Copyright © 2018 by Janet and Geoff Benge

Published by Emerald Books
P.O. Box 635
Lynnwood, WA 98046

All rights reserved. No part of this book may be reproduced in any form without permission in writing from the publisher, except in the case of brief quotations in critical articles or reviews.

Cataloging-in-Publication Data is on file at the Library of Congress.

ISBN 978-1-62486-123-9 (print)
ISBN 978-1-62486-130-7 (e-book)

First printing 2018

Printed in the United States of America

HEROES OF HISTORY

Abraham Lincoln
Alan Shepard
Ben Carson
Benjamin Franklin
Benjamin Rush
Billy Graham
Captain John Smith
Christopher Columbus
Clara Barton
Davy Crockett
Daniel Boone
Douglas MacArthur
Elizabeth Fry
Ernest Shackleton
George Washington
George Washington Carver
Harriet Tubman
John Adams
Laura Ingalls Wilder
Louis Zamperini
Meriwether Lewis
Milton Hershey
Orville Wright
Ronald Reagan
Theodore Roosevelt
Thomas Edison
William Bradford
William Penn
William Wilberforce

Available in paperback, e-book, and audiobook formats.
Unit Study Curriculum Guides are available for many biographies.
www.emeraldbooks.com

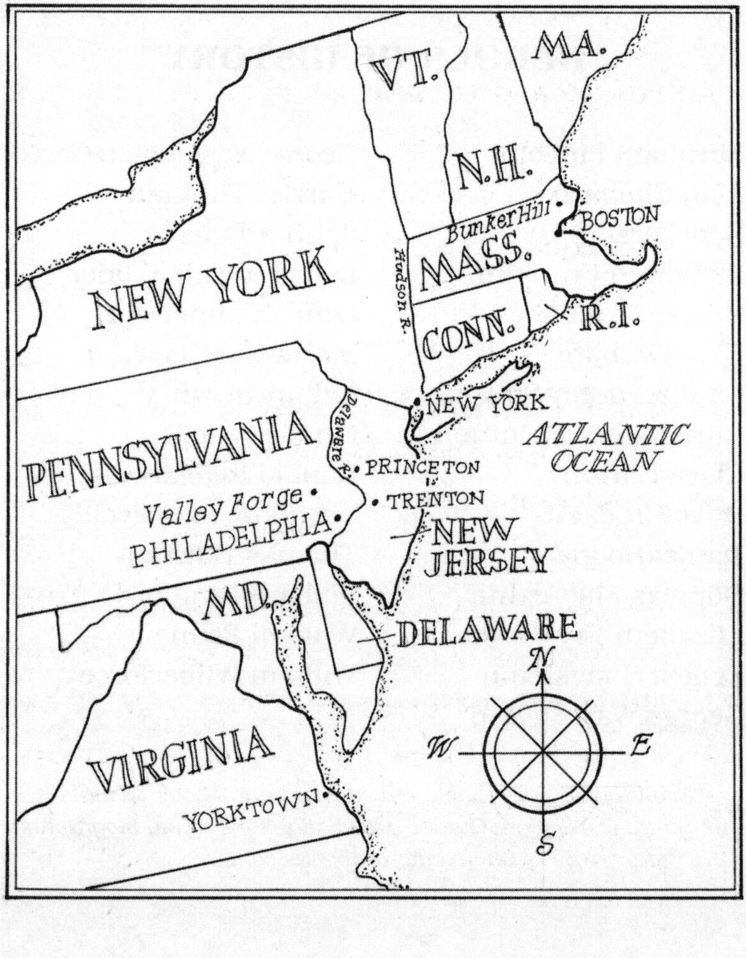

VT.
MA.
N.H.
Bunker Hill
BOSTON
MASS.
Hudson R.
NEW YORK
CONN.
R.I.
NEW YORK
ATLANTIC
OCEAN
PENNSYLVANIA
Delaware R.
PRINCETON
Valley Forge
TRENTON
PHILADELPHIA
NEW
JERSEY
MD.
DELAWARE
N
W
E
S
VIRGINIA
YORKTOWN

Contents

Chapter 1

Seasick and Terrified

The *Friendship* had barely cleared Cape Henlopen, Delaware, when Benjamin Rush began to feel a strange queasiness in his stomach. Beneath him the ship rolled gently on the swell. As the vessel headed farther out into the Atlantic Ocean, Ben became violently ill, constantly vomiting into a bucket or over the side of the ship. The last thing Ben wanted to do was eat, but Captain Pearse, the *Friendship*'s master, insisted he try to swallow some food, telling him that food in his stomach would help settle his seasickness. It didn't. Ben had taken only a few mouthfuls when he had to jump up from the table and run out on deck. He made it to the ship's side in time to throw up into the churning ocean.

For Ben, there was no more eating. Instead he lay on the bunk in his cabin or in a sunny corner of the deck during the day, feeling wretched. He had no idea a person could vomit so much. He was weak and depressed, as if a fog had descended over him. All he could focus on was how nauseated he felt. He was unable to force his mind to ponder the things that lay ahead for him on the other side of the Atlantic. Sometimes he doubted that he would even make it across.

It was ten days before the constant seasickness subsided and Ben started to find his sea legs. As he slowly began to eat a little and hold it down, he felt stronger. The nausea abated, and he found himself beginning to contemplate Scotland and what it held for him. For several days Ben enjoyed feeling normal. He basked in the sun when it shone and talked with his friends Johnathan Potts and James Cummins, marveling that neither of them had gotten seasick.

Then from out of nowhere, it seemed to Ben, the *Friendship* was enveloped by a howling gale. The ship's timbers creaked and groaned eerily, and the vessel pitched and rolled heavily in the mountainous surf whipped up by the wind. It wasn't seasickness that seized Ben this time. It was terror as the ship was buffeted by the angry ocean. Ben huddled in his berth below deck. He stayed there for three days while the storm raged. He expected the ship to break apart and sink at any moment.

The *Friendship* survived the storm, as did Ben. When the vessel stopped violently pitching and rolling, a weak and hungry Ben made his way up on deck. The sun was just breaking through the clouds, and Captain Pearse assured Ben that clear weather was ahead. Ben wasn't so sure. He sat down on a pile of coiled ropes and looked out across the gray ocean. He wondered why he'd allowed his thirst for more knowledge to entice him into boarding the *Friendship* in the first place. As a boy sitting by the docks in Philadelphia, watching ships come and go, he'd thought about what it must be like to be a sailor and travel to all sorts of exotic ports around the world. Now he knew, and it wasn't anything like he'd imagined. Right at that moment he wished he were back in Philadelphia with his feet on solid, dry land.

Chapter 2

Coming and Going

It was a sunny summer day in 1754 as eight-year-old Benjamin Rush sat on a piling by Carpenter's Wharf at the end of Walnut Street. He watched sailors climbing the rigging and patching sails. He listened to the chanting of slaves as they stowed ships' holds with sacks of corn and wheat or rolled barrels of molasses down gangplanks. As he watched, Ben thought about his older brother James, who had recently gone to sea. As far as Ben could tell, his mother believed this would cure some kind of problem James had. Ben wasn't sure what the problem was, just that it made his brother moody.

Now James was working aboard a ship that sailed between England, Africa, and North America, the "triangle of trade," as another uncle told Ben the route was called. Ben's uncle explained that textiles, rum, and manufactured goods were shipped from England to Africa. Once the ship had unloaded in Africa, it was loaded with slaves to be transported to North America. After the slaves were delivered, the ship was loaded with corn, wheat, dried meats, wood, tobacco, and molasses bound for England, where the cycle started over again. Philadelphia, the largest port in Britain's North American colonies, bustled with activity. Ben took every opportunity he could to head down to the docks and watch the ships.

Today, as Ben watched the waterfront activity, his mind drifted to the future. His mother had just told him that he and his younger brother Jacob would be leaving home in August. The two were being sent off to attend West Nottingham Academy, sixty miles southwest of Philadelphia, just across the Pennsylvania border in Maryland. Going so far from home wasn't too scary for Ben, since the principal of the academy was his uncle, the Reverend Samuel Finley. Samuel was married to Ben's mother's younger sister, Sarah. Ben and Jacob would be staying at the Finleys' house while they attended the school. Not only that, Uncle Samuel and Aunt Sarah had eight children who all lived at home, and Ben looked forward to spending time with his cousins.

Looking over the Delaware River, Ben realized how much he would miss Philadelphia and its fifteen thousand inhabitants. He loved strolling along the streets, buying produce for his mother at the market, and watching ships load and unload. On his walks he would pass cobblers, wig makers, barbers, and cabinetmakers, all busy plying their trades. On foggy days, he would miss the sound of the bells and horns that guided ships up the Delaware River to Philadelphia's docks.

Later that day Ben's mother, Susanna, walked with him and Jacob to Christ Church Cemetery, where their father had been buried three years before. Ben had been five then, and he remembered the breeze that blew off the river that July day during the service. John Rush had gotten sick and died quickly. His last words were, "Lord, Lord, Lord." Ben thought the utterance fitting. His father had been a strong Christian man who was looked up to in the community for his honesty and hard work. Just weeks after his father's death, Ben's baby brother John died from a fever. He was buried beside his father.

John Rush had been a gunsmith. He wasn't originally from the city. He was born and raised on the Rush family farm in Byberry along the Delaware River, fifteen miles north of Philadelphia. That was where Ben had also been born. When Ben was two, his family moved from the farm into Philadelphia so that Ben's father could set up a gunsmith business. When Ben's father died, his mother sold his father's tools, some property they'd owned, and all but one of the family slaves. With the money, she bought a general store on High Street, just east of Second Street. The store, which she named the Blazing Star, sold liquor, supplies, and staples such as flour, sugar, molasses, and dried fruit. Ben knew that his mother had worked hard to build up the business, which was now quite successful. Even as a widow, she'd made enough money to send Ben and Jacob off to school.

As he packed his clothes, Ben wasn't sure how he felt about going away to school. Living in the country had its good points—Ben liked hunting and fishing—but he knew he would miss his mother and his two older sisters, Rachel and Rebecca, who lived at home and helped their mother run the Blazing Star. Yet Ben knew he needed a good education. All his relatives said so, and he had hundreds of relatives.

Ben's mother had told him he was probably related to every Rush he met in Pennsylvania. That was because his great-great grandfather, John Rush, had come from England and settled in Pennsylvania soon after the colony's founding. This John Rush, whom the family referred to as Old Trooper, seemed to Ben to be a heroic character. He was captain of a horse brigade in the Puritan army during England's Civil War. He helped Oliver Cromwell overthrow King Charles I and replace the monarchy with a new form of government—first the Commonwealth of England from 1649 to 1653 and then the Protectorate until 1659.

Hanging above the front door in the Rush home was Old Trooper's sword. Ben was sure that his great-great grandfather had killed people with it. Sometimes Ben's mother let him and Jacob take it down to clean it, though they weren't allowed to play with it—it was sharp and heavy.

Old Trooper was sixty-three years old when he decided he'd had enough of England. As a Quaker, he was tired of the constant persecution he and other Quakers endured, especially after the reestablishment of the monarchy in 1660 and the return of Charles II from exile in Europe to rule. In 1683, Old Trooper convinced his entire family to leave England for America to participate in William Penn's "Holy Experiment." The Holy Experiment revolved around the establishment of a new American colony in which Quakers and other religious minorities could live in harmony and free from persecution. The new colony was called Pennsylvania after its founder.

John Rush, his six sons, his two daughters, and their spouses and children made the six-week voyage across the Atlantic Ocean to Pennsylvania. They settled on a five-hundred-acre land grant at Byberry, upriver from newly founded Philadelphia. That was over seventy years ago, and now the Rush family was spread far and wide. Some were still farmers in and around Byberry, others were tradesmen, and a few were scholars. The latter was what Ben's mother had told him he should be. Ben had a quick mind and a powerful memory, she said, two important things a doctor, lawyer, or clergyman needed.

Ben wasn't sure he wanted to be any of those things. Besides, at eight years of age, how could he possibly know what he wanted? He liked to study hard, and until now his mother had supervised his learning, drilling him on his multiplication tables and on the names of the various states and kingdoms in Europe. While Ben enjoyed learning from his mother, she told him West Nottingham Academy was too good an opportunity to miss, especially since he would be studying under such a well-respected scholar as Uncle Samuel.

A week later Ben and Jacob were delivered by stagecoach to West Nottingham Academy. Ben took with him his fishing rod and a rifle his father had made—two essential items for a boy living in the country.

Ben and Jacob were welcomed into the Finley home and soon settled into school. Uncle Samuel taught them and the other twenty-eight boys Latin, Greek, philosophy, mathematics, and composition, along with religion. Luckily, Ben found religion an interesting topic. When his father was alive, the family attended Christ Church in Philadelphia, an Anglican church. After his death, their mother had transferred them all to Second Presbyterian Church. There Ben had listened to sermons from some of the great preachers inspired by George Whitefield and the Great Awakening. In fact, Uncle Samuel had been the church's first pastor. But Samuel had left the church to start West Nottingham Academy, training up boys from the American colonies to study at the College of New Jersey. This was one of four colleges in the American colonies, and the only Presbyterian one. The aim of the College of New Jersey was to raise up American-born Presbyterian pastors who understood the importance of the Great Awakening and the challenges of life in the colonies.

Fitting in at West Nottingham Academy was easy for Ben. He loved talking with his classmates and the constant stream of interesting people who shared the family's supper table. One of Uncle Samuel's favorite sayings was "Conversation is education," and he invited preachers, travelers, and adventurers to dine with the boys.

The boys attending the academy lived in a dormitory wing of the house, but Ben and Jacob lived with their cousins and participated in Finley family life. Religion was an important part of their lives. Each morning Uncle Samuel read aloud a chapter from the Bible and explained its meaning. On Sundays after church, Ben and his cousins took turns reciting back to Uncle Samuel as much of the sermon as they could remember. Ben could often recite long passages word for word.

Because Uncle Samuel believed that the academy should be as self-sufficient as possible, all the boys helped with the farmwork while keeping up their studies. There were cows to milk, a vegetable garden to weed, and crops to harvest, and studies were even interrupted at haymaking time. Ben enjoyed these outdoor pursuits, though not as much as hunting and fishing, which he did every chance he got.

At Christmas, Ben and Jacob were allowed to return home to Philadelphia for a few days. During Christmas 1756, Ben wasn't very enthusiastic about one change that had occurred at home. His mother had remarried a local distiller named Richard Morris, whom Ben did not like very much. However, Ben could do little about it. He was glad to get back to West Nottingham Academy after Christmas.

Four years of study at the academy flew by, and before Ben knew it, he was twelve years old and ready to move on to college. The College of Philadelphia seemed the most convenient school for Ben to attend, except for the fact that it was run by the Church of England. Ben's mother firmly believed that he should be educated at a Presbyterian college, which meant the College of New Jersey at Princeton. When Ben sat the college's entrance exams, Uncle Samuel's tutelage at West Nottingham Academy paid off. Not only did Ben pass the exams, but he did so well that he was allowed to skip the first two years and enter the college as a junior. Ben looked forward to the start of this new stage of his life.

Chapter 3

Choosing a Career

On a bright sunny morning in 1758, Ben climbed down from the stagecoach and surveyed his new home, Nassau Hall in Princeton, New Jersey. He was in awe of the size of Nassau Hall, which he had been told was the largest stone building in all North America. It had been erected three years before to hold about one hundred students, along with faculty. Ben was greeted by the College of New Jersey's acting president, the Reverend Jacob Green. The previous president, Jonathan Edwards, had died from an experimental smallpox inoculation after just two months in the position.

Ben was one of the youngest among the fifty students attending the college, but he knew he would fit in well. Many of the other students had also been taught at West Nottingham Academy. Ben was especially glad to see Ebenezer Hazard. The two had been good friends at the academy.

Each day at the College of New Jersey started at 5:30 a.m. with the clanging of the bell in the cupola. This was followed by a servant pounding on the door of the dormitory room Ben shared with two other juniors. The entire college then gathered for prayer in a spacious room with two-story vaulted ceilings. Prayer was followed by an hour of study, and then came breakfast. Lectures were held from nine in the morning until one in the afternoon and covered Latin, Greek, literature, and mathematics. The rest of the day consisted of lunch, more prayer, study, supper, and bed. Ben had grown used to a similar routine at West Nottingham Academy and adapted easily.

Two months after Ben started attending the college, everything changed. A new president arrived at the College of New Jersey. His name was Samuel Davies, and Ben liked him immediately. The thirty-five-year-old president was the son of a Delaware farmer and had risen to become one of the best-loved non-Anglican preachers in the American colonies. He often spoke about the right of all people to follow their conscience in religious matters.

Ben was captivated by the stories Samuel Davies told about the years he had spent riding a five-hundred-mile circuit through the backwoods of Virginia, and especially about how he'd preached to thousands of slaves. Samuel had interesting views on slavery, arguing that a black slave was just as intelligent as a white slave owner. The only difference, he said, was that the white person was likelier to have had a formal education. Ben's family had always owned slaves to help on the farm and at the gunsmith shop when his father was alive. Still, Ben hadn't given any thought to how, given different circumstances, a black person might have grown up to be just like him.

Much to Ben's delight, Samuel was more interested in poetry, composition, and public speaking than he was in Latin and Greek. He insisted that every student learn to harangue, or argue well. Ben excelled at debating, and the new president took a genuine interest in his development.

Samuel also encouraged the boys to keep a commonplace book, a notebook in which they could record anything they found interesting. Ben loved this idea and quickly filled his first commonplace book with notes on his studies, hymns and poems he liked, words of wisdom from his lecturers, and snippets of news he heard.

It wasn't easy to get an accurate account of what was going on in the other American colonies. However, Ben tried his best to keep up with the war between the British and the French on the outer edges of the colonies. When the French began expanding their territorial control into the Ohio River Valley, they came into direct conflict with the British colonies, who also laid claim to this territory. This had led to a series of skirmishes between the French and their Indian allies and the British and colonial militias. In 1756 the British officially declared war against France in North America. Ben tried to learn as much as he could about how the war, which had been going on for two years now, was progressing. Apparently in England, a statesman named William Pitt had convinced Parliament to increase the money committed to fighting the war. Ben learned that this increase in funding was helping the British turn the tide against the French forces. Samuel Davies was a strong supporter of the British forces fighting the war. He actively recruited many young men to fight with the British against the French and the Indians.

At college, Ben studied hard and made good grades in all his subjects, moving quickly from one class to the next. As he progressed, he knew he would soon have to choose a career. His mother had made many sacrifices for him to get an education, and like most of the other college students, he would be expected to choose a career in law, medicine, or the church.

Even though Ben was a devout Presbyterian, he could not see himself as a pastor. Nor could he see himself as a doctor. He hated the sight of blood and vomit—two things doctors saw a lot of. Samuel Davies encouraged him to go into law, explaining to Ben that he was one of the top orators in the college and had a clear mind. Ben had to agree. Being a lawyer sounded like a profession where he could excel. He wrote to his mother and asked her to find him an apprenticeship with a lawyer in Philadelphia after he graduated.

Soon afterward, Ben received a letter in reply saying his mother would search out an apprenticeship for him. But her letter also brought sad news:

Ben's twenty-year-old brother James had died of yellow fever on a ship off the coast of Jamaica.

On September 21, 1760, Benjamin Rush sat with his graduating class at the College of New Jersey, taking in all that Samuel Davies was saying in his valedictory address.

> Permit me, my dear Youth, to inculcate upon you this important Instruction, imbibe and cherish a Publick Spirit. Serve your Generation. Live not for your selves, but the Publick. Be the Servants of the Church, the Servants of your country, the Servants of all. Extend the Arms of your Benevolence to embrace your Friends, your Neighbors, your Country, your Nation, the whole Race of Mankind, even your Enemies. Let it be the vigorous unremitted Effort of your whole life, to leave the World wiser and better, than you found it at your Entrance. Esteem yourselves by so much the more happy, honorable and important, by how much the more useful you are. . . . Let your own Pleasure, your own private Interests, yield to the common Good. For this, spare no Pains; avoid no labor; dread no Sufferings. For this, *do* every Thing; *suffer* every Thing. For this, live and die. From this, let no selfish Passion mislead you; no ungrateful Returns, the useful Returns of active Benevolence, discourage you; let no Opposition deter you; no private Interest bribe you. To this, be your Bodies, your Souls, your Estates, your Life,

your All sacred. Bravely live and die, serving your *Generation*—your *own* Generation. . . .

Do not imagine, you may now put an End to your Studies, as having arrived to the utmost Limits of useful Knowledge. A College-Education does only lay the Foundation; on which to build, must be the Business of your future Life. If you neglect this, even the Foundation however skillfully laid, will gradually moulder away. You will live your Age *backward;* and be less wise at Sixty, than at Twenty. . . .

And now, my ever-dear Pupils, I must dismiss you from my Care, into the wide World, to shift for yourselves. You enter into it with the great Advantage of a fair Character; for I must do you the Justice to declare, that you have always been dutiful teachable Pupils to me; and this whole House can attest the regularity of your general Conduct, since you have been Members of it. Go on in this Path; and may it shine more and more till the perfect Day!

Farewell! My dear young Friends.

When the valedictory address and graduation ceremony were over, Ben walked down the stone steps of Nassau Hall and out onto the front lawn. He felt proud of himself. He was fourteen years old and had earned a Bachelor of Arts degree. A bright future in law lay ahead of him, or so he thought.

Before returning to Philadelphia, Ben visited his aunt, uncle, and cousins at West Nottingham Academy, where he talked with current students about his experiences at college and encouraged them to work hard.

On the day he was due to leave, Uncle Samuel called Ben into his office. "What are your plans now?" he asked.

"I am planning to enter law," Ben replied. "My mother has already found a lawyer to apprentice me to."

"I can see how that would use many of your talents," his uncle said. "But I would urge you to think again. The practice of law is full of temptations. I think you should consider medicine."

Ben's heart sank. He respected Uncle Samuel immensely, but he couldn't see himself as a doctor. A doctor's life did not appeal to him one bit.

"I can see it's not appealing to you," Uncle Samuel continued, "but before you determine anything, set aside a day for fasting and prayer and ask God to direct you in your choice of a profession."

As Ben sat in the stagecoach on the journey back to Philadelphia, he didn't fast and pray, but he did think hard about what his uncle had said. Would medicine be a better choice for him? Ben didn't know, but he did know that the decision was an important one. Both law and medicine required a five-year apprenticeship, and whichever direction he chose to go, he would be bonded to a lawyer or a doctor until he was nearly twenty years old.

Ben wrestled with the question. He wished he could ask his father what to do, as many of the other graduating students had, but his father had died a long time ago. As the stagecoach rocked from side to side, Ben began thinking about death. He had vague memories of his father and his youngest brother, John, dying. Tears sprang to his eyes as he thought of his older brother, James, lying ill with yellow fever on a ship in the Caribbean before he died. What kind of medical treatment had he received?

And what about yellow fever? Thousands of people died from the disease each year, but what caused it and how did people catch it? Was there some undiscovered medicine or procedure that could prevent the disease? The more Ben thought about these questions, the more he realized he wanted to answer them. Law was a good profession, and Ben knew that he had many skills that would make him a good lawyer. But lawyers weren't engaged in finding lifesaving answers to the kinds of questions he was thinking about. Ben realized he wanted to play a part in finding these answers, despite his aversion to the sight of blood and vomit. It was too late to save his father and brothers, but perhaps he could save the lives of many other people.

Chapter 4

Apprentice

On February 4, 1761, a month after his fifteenth birthday, Ben sat in Dr. John Redman's office. A maid had shown him in, and as he waited for the doctor to return from his afternoon rounds, he looked around. The office walls were lined with medical books—some in English, others in Latin. This was as Ben had expected. Dr. Redman had a reputation for being the most thoroughly trained doctor in Pennsylvania, if not in all the American colonies. He had crammed a lot into thirty-nine years of life. John Redman had been an apprentice doctor in Philadelphia and had practiced medicine in Bermuda before going on to study at the two most famous medical schools in the world: the University of Edinburgh in Scotland and Leyden University in Holland. After earning his medical degree, he had worked in Paris and London before returning to Philadelphia, where he established a successful medical practice.

A short while later, the door to the doctor's office swung open. "Ah, there you are, lad," a short, dark-haired man said.

Ben stood and bowed.

"Sit down, sit down," Dr. Redman instructed. "Mr. Finley wrote telling me that you're a fine young scholar just graduated from the College of New Jersey and that you wish to be apprenticed to me."

"Yes, sir," Ben answered. "I should like that very much."

"Tell me some more about yourself," the doctor said.

Although Ben had dreaded being asked such questions, he felt at ease with Dr. Redman and told him a little about his family. He explained that his two older sisters had recently married, that he was the oldest living son, and that his father had died when he was five years old.

"And what of your religious training at college? Did you heed the teaching of Samuel Davies?" John Redman asked.

Ben smiled. "Yes, sir. I was raised in the Presbyterian faith, and I count it my greatest joy to read the Bible and meditate upon it."

"That's what I like to hear from an apprentice," the doctor said with a nod. "Knowledge and discipline help make a man more useful, but faith in God alone can make us happy in ourselves, a real blessing to our generation. Being a doctor resembles a pastor's life in many ways. You must spend every hour engaged in doing good to both the rich and the poor, relieving the suffering of fellow mortals, and perhaps receiving daily thanks from those who are ready to perish."

"Yes, sir," Ben replied. "The Reverend Davies told us in his valedictory sermon that we are to strive to better the lot of others, and I wish to commit my life to doing that."

"Very well," Dr. Redman said. "I'm in need of a new apprentice. My last one, John Morgan, has left to take his degree in Edinburgh. I'll send the papers home with you. Your mother can sign for you. I'll expect you back here in the morning to start. Bring your clothes and bedding with you. And your Latin books. Get some rest. There will be plenty to do tomorrow. You'll start out in the apothecary shop."

Ben whistled as he walked home, down Walnut Street and past the red brick Pennsylvania State House. Like many of the shops and buildings in the city, it was still draped in black crepe, a sign of mourning for the death of King George II of England. The king had been dead for six weeks before news finally reached the residents of Pennsylvania. Old King George was the only king Ben had ever known. It felt strange to now have a new king, King George III. Ben wondered what change, if any, the new king would make for the American colonies.

When Ben arrived home, his mother met him at the door with a newspaper in her hand. "You'd better sit down," she said.

Ben frowned. What could have happened that was more important than his interview with Dr. Redman?

"It's Samuel Davies. He's gone," his mother said, laying the newspaper on the table in front of her son.

Ben stared at the headline. "College of New Jersey President Is Dead." It was difficult for him to believe that the man who'd had such an influence on his life had died at just thirty-seven years of age. Ben knew he would miss his old college president.

That night Susanna Rush signed the official papers binding Ben to Dr. John Redman to be his apprentice for the next five years. Ben would live in Dr. Redman's house, obey his rules, and learn all he could about medicine from the doctor. Although Ben wouldn't get paid for the time he was an apprentice, he knew it was an honor to be trained by such a well-respected man.

Ben's first job was to acquaint himself with the apothecary, the room at the rear of the house where he would grind medical compounds, fill pill bottles, and steep herbal remedies. Ben realized that he had a lot to learn. Medical cures tended to come from a mixture of drugs, many of which arrived by ship from England. Local cures involved such methods as using tulip tree bark to treat snakebites, cooking marigold flowers in pig fat to make ointment, and boiling sassafras root to make a healing tonic. In fact, the sassafras root tonic had proved so successful that it was also bottled and exported to Europe.

Ben soon discovered that there were few written instructions on how to mix various medicines, and the instructions that did exist were so vague as to be almost useless. Nonetheless, he pressed on. He started with simples, medicines with only one active ingredient. The next step was learning to mix compounds, which combined two or more active ingredients. These ingredients could be boiled together, steeped, or ground with a mortar and pestle. Tinctures were the most difficult to produce. When an ingredient would not dissolve in water, it was dissolved in alcohol, creating a tincture. Ben had no exact measuring spoons to use as he mixed the medicines. A previous apprentice had left instructions such as "enough opium to lie on a penknife point" and a "pretty draught of mercury." Ben had to experiment with how much these quantities might be.

As he learned the art of mixing medicines in the apothecary, Ben was amazed at some of the "cures" patients tried before coming to Dr. Redman. One patient, whose foot had been trodden on by a galloping horse, had treated his injury by smearing cow dung over it. A man with a knife wound had covered it with rabbit fat.

Besides working in the apothecary, Ben had other jobs. One was washing the equipment in Dr. Redman's medical bag each night and restocking the bag in the morning with the clean equipment and supplies. As he wiped the bloodletting lancet, pewter bowl, and glass cups, Ben dreaded the day when he would accompany Dr. Redman on his visits to patients and use the instruments to bleed people himself.

As an apprentice, Ben became a part of the Redman household. After dinner, Dr. Redman would drill him on what he had read the night before and assign him new areas to study. The doctor's favorite topic was "making sense of medicine." He often talked with Ben about the importance of not just treating symptoms but also understanding where illness came from. To explain this thoroughly, he gave Ben two books, one by Dr. Thomas Sydenham and the other by Dr. Herman Boerhaave. Both books were written in Latin, and Ben read them carefully, making notes in his commonplace book as he read.

Thomas Sydenham, an English doctor who'd died seventy years before, explained how all diseases in the body were the result of "morbific matter," or disease-causing matter. This morbific matter circulated in the blood of sick people and permeated their tissue. The first step in curing a patient was to get as much of this matter from the body as possible. To do this, medicines were used to induce vomiting, diarrhea, and sweating. Doctors were also encouraged to cut open a patient's vein and let as much blood bleed out as possible. Once as much liquid as possible had been released from the body, the patient was told to rest, eat only small amounts of food, and get lots of fresh air.

Dr. Herman Boerhaave built his book on Dr. Sydenham's ideas. He was a Dutchman who had taught at the University of Leyden for forty-two years, dying shortly before John Redman studied there. To Dr. Boerhaave, the body was like a complicated water-pumping system. In his book, he talked about pipes and valves and the volume of all kinds of liquids flowing throughout the body. He believed that when the blood flowed too fast, it caused friction on the artery walls, which led to fever. It made perfect sense to Ben when he read about Boerhaave's theory that a sick person's pulse often raced wildly. Ben noted in his commonplace book, "Bleeding is proper at the onset of all inflammatory illnesses. It is likewise proper in all topical inflammations, as those of the intestines, womb, bladder, stomach, kidneys . . . rheumatism, the apoplexy, epilepsy, and the bloody flux. After falls, blows, bruises, or any violent hurt received either externally or internally, bleeding is necessary."

Some doctors still used leeches to suck blood out of sick patients, but this approach was considered old-fashioned, since it was difficult to know exactly how much blood the leeches had sucked up. Cupping was now considered the modern approach to reducing the volume of a patient's blood. Ben knew it wouldn't be long before he was expected to use this approach to bleed people.

A year after Ben started his apprenticeship, Dr. Redman accepted a new apprentice, Sam Treat, who took over in the apothecary. This allowed Ben to continue to the next stage of learning to become a doctor—accompanying Dr. Redman on his visits to patients in their homes.

The first patient Ben and Dr. Redman visited had a rash and a fever, the perfect combination of symptoms for bleeding. Ben watched as Dr. Redman took a bell-shaped glass cup from his bag and warmed it under a candle. The doctor then placed the cup on the woman's forearm and continued to hold the candle near it. The difference in heat created a vacuum inside the bell-shaped glass cup, causing the skin to pull up. Dr. Redman explained that this made the next step in the process easier and helped to relieve some of the pain the patient would feel. The doctor then removed the glass cup and cut into the woman's vein with a lancet. Blood began to flow from the vein into a pewter bowl. Watching the procedure wasn't as bad as Ben thought it would be. He reminded himself how much Dr. Redman was helping the patient by bleeding her.

Soon Ben was able to accompany John Redman on his rounds in Pennsylvania Hospital, where Dr. Redman was a consulting physician. Pennsylvania Hospital, the first hospital in the American colonies, had been founded in 1751 by Benjamin Franklin and Dr. Thomas Bond. Most of the patients treated at the hospital were poor, aged, or mentally ill, and the place smelled so bad that Ben gagged upon entering. Anyone with money or family would surely want to be treated at home, and not in a place like the hospital.

Ben followed Dr. Redman as he went from patient to patient. The doctor would bleed some people, cut away ulcerous sores on others, pull rotten teeth, and perform amputations. On his first visit, Ben even got to assist the doctor as he performed surgery to remove bladder stones. Thankfully, the patient survived. In about 40 percent of the cases, Dr. Redman explained, the patient did not.

Besides accompanying the doctor as he visited patients, Ben was entrusted with collecting fees and keeping Dr. Redman's account books up-to-date.

In 1762 a smallpox epidemic swept through Philadelphia, and Dr. Redman began carrying an extra supply of tobacco in his medical case. "Put a large ball of it in your mouth before seeing a patient," he told Ben. "The tobacco absorbs all of your saliva, preventing you from swallowing it and catching the ague [illness] yourself. Also, never visit a smallpox patient on an empty stomach," he warned.

Ben helped Dr. Redman as he went from home to home. The doctor recommended purifying the air in the rooms of sick people by plunging a hot iron into a bowl of vinegar. He also handed out laxatives to help the disease exit the body as quickly as possible. Many patients suffering from smallpox were also bled, especially pregnant women. Ben was told they particularly benefited from the procedure.

No sooner had the smallpox outbreak subsided than yellow fever broke out in Philadelphia. The epidemic seemed to hit hardest those living along Dock Creek, the edge of the Delaware River, and some marshland to the south. Ben recorded in his commonplace book the number of patients who were dying from the disease. The outbreak began in late August and reached its peak in the fourth week of September, when twenty people died each day from yellow fever.

Dr. Redman tried hard to come up with a reason why yellow fever struck the area, as it usually did around this time of year. He concluded that the disease had been imported to Philadelphia from Savannah, Georgia, by a sailor, and that it was spreading from person to person through touch. The doctor also told Ben that as in other years, the yellow fever would subside when the first frost of the fall arrived. Sure enough, it did.

Shortly after the end of the epidemic, Dr. Redman showed Ben a notice in the *Pennsylvania Gazette*, announcing that Dr. William Shippen Jr. was to offer a course of lectures on anatomy in the State House. The lectures were open to medical students and doctors' apprentices. They were also offered for "the entertainment of any gentleman who may have the curiosity to understand the Anatomy of the Human Frame." Dr. Redman encouraged Ben to attend.

Ben knew of William Shippen Jr. He was a graduate of Uncle Samuel's West Nottingham Academy and the College of New Jersey, and he had just returned from Edinburgh after completing his medical degree. His father, William Shippen Sr., was a Philadelphia doctor.

Thus far in his medical apprenticeship, Ben had learned little about anatomy and the layout of internal organs and structures in the body. He attended William Shippen Jr.'s opening lecture at the State House along with ten other medical apprentices and several doctors.

During the lecture, William Jr. used anatomical drawings to illustrate what he was saying. He also used plaster casts to demonstrate the structures and functions of various parts of the body. Ben was amazed by the drawings, which were detailed and elaborate, unlike the drawings he'd seen in medical books.

Ben returned for Dr. Shippen's next two lectures. Then, at the fourth lecture, Dr. Shippen announced, "By some means we must secure a corpse to dissect." Ben, like most of the others present in the room, gasped. The idea that a doctor, medical student, or apprentice might learn about the inner workings of the body by dissecting a cadaver was frowned upon in the American colonies. Many found it disrespectful to treat the body of a human being this way. But William Jr. was undeterred. Two weeks later he had secured the body of a runaway slave who'd died in jail. Since he wasn't allowed to dissect the body in the State House, the lectures moved to a small laboratory behind Dr. William Shippen Sr.'s brick home in Philadelphia.

Ben was shocked at first when he walked in and saw the cadaver, covered by a sheet, lying on a table in the center of the room. Once everyone arrived for the lecture, William Jr. pulled back the sheet with a flourish to reveal the dead body. He then began moving the cadaver's arms and legs to explain how they worked. He was just about to pick up his knife and start the dissection when a commotion erupted. "Murderer! Grave robber!" came shouts from outside. Through the window Ben could see a group of angry men. They pelted the building with rocks and held lighted torches, trying to set the place afire.

William Shippen Jr. told those who'd come to the lecture to guard the door and windows while he stepped outside to confront the mob. Ben could hear him trying to reason with them, but they refused to be placated. Instead they began throwing their torches in the direction of the laboratory. Thankfully, as Ben peered out the window, no one seemed to have good aim, and the burning torches landed on the ground. The tension was suddenly broken when William Shippen's father and a group of police officers burst into the backyard. The mob fled.

After peace was restored, the dissection went ahead. Dr. Shippen Jr. cut into the cadaver to reveal various body organs and explain how they functioned. Although Ben had assisted Dr. Redman with the amputation of legs and arms and had even helped remove bladder stones, he was shocked when William Shippen cut into the chest of the dead body. But as William Jr. peeled back the skin and muscle tissue and spread the ribs to reveal the heart and lungs, Ben had to admit that the inner workings of the human body were truly amazing. He returned for all of William Shippen Jr.'s remaining lectures, hoping to learn as much as he could.

Chapter 5

Edinburgh

During the winter of 1762–63, word reached the American colonies that England and France had signed the Treaty of Paris. This was a peace agreement that ended the French and Indian War that had dragged on for seven years. Ben, like most colonists, was glad the war was over. Under the treaty terms, Great Britain and France each returned territory they'd captured during the war, though since the British were considered victors in the fighting, they also gained control of many of France's North American possessions.

Meanwhile, Ben's medical apprenticeship continued. There were times when Dr. Redman fell ill and Ben had to take over the medical practice as best he could. Then in the winter of 1764, Ben himself became ill. He began coughing up blood and assumed he had consumption, a lung disease that killed a hundred or more residents of Philadelphia each year. John Redman bled Ben several times and changed Ben's diet to mainly vegetables and tea and coffee. The treatment seemed to work, and before long Ben started to feel better.

During 1765, the last year of Ben's medical apprenticeship, Dr. John Morgan, John Redman's thirty-year-old former apprentice, returned to Philadelphia. Like William Shippen Jr., he had attended West Nottingham Academy and was a graduate of the College of New Jersey. After his apprenticeship, John Morgan had spent five years earning his medical degree at Edinburgh University. Together, William Shippen Jr. and John Morgan had plans to open a medical school at the College of Philadelphia. They hoped this would greatly improve the quality of American doctors and eliminate the need to travel to Europe for advanced medical study. Before leaving England, John Morgan had sought out Thomas Penn, proprietor of Pennsylvania colony and son of its founder William Penn, and received his permission to set up the new medical school.

Once the new medical school was established at the College of Philadelphia, John Morgan and William Shippen Jr. began arguing over which of them was more qualified to take up the new lecturing position at the college. Ben tried not to take sides in the matter, but the disagreement between the two men blossomed into an all-out feud. In the end, the trustees of the College of Philadelphia chose John Morgan to head the medical school and be its chief lecturer. However, as a gesture to William Shippen Jr., they made him the new school's anatomy lecturer.

During that year, Great Britain decided that the American colonists should pay for their own defense. Although the French and Indian War had ended two years earlier, King George III complained that waging war in North America cost a lot of money, most of it paid by Great Britain. Parliament in London left ten thousand British troops stationed in the American wilderness. Members of Parliament reasoned that this was to protect the colonists, but many colonists believed it was just a cheap place to house the British army until another war broke out somewhere else in Great Britain's growing empire. Nonetheless, Parliament decided that since the American colonists were benefiting from the outcome of the war and the ongoing protection of the British army, they should start paying for the cost of the war and having the soldiers in their midst.

On November 1, 1765, word reached Philadelphia that Parliament had passed the Stamp Act. Ben soon learned that this act imposed a tax on virtually every paper product sold in the American colonies. If something didn't have the proper stamp affixed to it, it was illegal. Everything made of paper—from shipping bills to newspapers, wills, contracts, even playing cards—was taxed. Ben had never been particularly interested in politics before this. During his childhood, things in Pennsylvania had been stable and predictable. Now it shocked him to realize that Parliament and the king could reach across the Atlantic Ocean and into the colonists' pockets. It was especially frustrating to Ben that the British were taxing things like newspapers and pamphlets, which many colonists used to educate themselves.

The Stamp Act affected everything and everyone in some way. Ben's younger brother Jacob graduated from the College of New Jersey and was forced to pay a tax on his diploma. And now that Jacob was apprenticed to a lawyer, he would have to pay a hefty tax to get his law license.

Ben felt bitterness creep into his heart over what was happening. As he talked to other colonists, he realized that many of them felt the same way. Arguments broke out as to how to deal with the matter. Some, like the Quakers, didn't want to challenge Parliament or King George III, but many others did. Samuel Adams, an influential legislator in Boston, Massachusetts, argued that the Stamp Act was unconstitutional. He supported a boycott of British goods to pressure Parliament into repealing the act. Something about Sam Adams's arguments stirred Ben's heart, and Ben had a feeling things weren't going to settle down in the American colonies anytime soon.

Despite the establishment of the new medical school at the College of Philadelphia, Ben's plan at the completion of his apprenticeship was to travel to Great Britain to pursue further medical studies. Instead of setting out immediately, however, he decided to spend a few more months working with John Redman.

In March 1766, after months of widespread protest throughout the American colonies and an impassioned appeal by Benjamin Franklin acting as an agent for the colonies, Parliament voted to repeal the Stamp Act. Ben was delighted with the outcome. It demonstrated the power of the colonists in North America when they acted together for a noble cause.

Ben continued working alongside Dr. Redman throughout the early months of 1766. He continued visiting and treating patients when the doctor was out of town for extended periods. It was during one of John Redman's absences that Ben had to treat his uncle Samuel. Back in 1761, following the death of the Reverend Samuel Davies, Samuel Finley became the fifth president of the College of New Jersey. At the beginning of July, Uncle Samuel fell gravely ill, and Ben was called in to tend to him. Ben did all he could, but nothing seemed to improve his uncle's condition. William Shippen Jr. was later called in to consult regarding Uncle Samuel's treatment. Still, nothing seemed to work. Dr. Shippen delivered the news to Ben that his Uncle Samuel had only a matter of days to live. Ben called the Finley family together and sat with his uncle day and night. He tried to make him as comfortable as possible. But at one o'clock in the morning on July 17, 1766, Samuel Finley died at the age of fifty-one.

For Ben, the death of his uncle brought back distant memories of the deaths of his father and of Samuel Davies. Despite his sadness, Ben kept busy. Only six weeks were left before he was to depart Philadelphia for England. He had booked passage to Liverpool aboard the *Friendship*, and from there he planned to travel two hundred miles overland to Edinburgh, Scotland.

Time passed quickly as Ben said goodbye to family and friends. On August 31, 1766, he and his friend Johnathan Potts, who also planned to study medicine in Edinburgh, set sail on the *Friendship*.

Johnathan came from a wealthy Quaker family that owned coal mines, furnaces, and forges in and around Pottsgrove, Pennsylvania. He and Ben, who were both twenty years old, met at one of Dr. John Morgan's lectures. At the dock, the two men met another young traveler, a Scotsman named James Cummins. James was a planter who'd lost all his money in the West Indies and was returning home to Great Britain on the *Friendship*.

Ben, who'd never been to sea before, was concerned about becoming seasick on the voyage. He soon discovered he'd been right to be concerned. No sooner had the *Friendship* cleared Cape Henlopen, Delaware, than Ben became violently seasick, a condition that lasted ten days. He was just beginning to feel better when the ship was overtaken by a huge gale. When the storm was over three days later, a weak and hungry Ben emerged from his berth.

On October 21, 1766, after seven weeks and two days crossing the Atlantic Ocean, the *Friendship* sailed into the bustling port of Liverpool. The size of the place astounded Ben. Captain Pearse of the *Friendship* laughed and explained that the port could accommodate three hundred ships. As they docked in Liverpool, Ben realized that many of those ships held slaves. The enormity of the slave trade shocked him. It is an "inhuman practice that men should grow rich by the calamities of their fellow creatures!" he wrote in his journal after his arrival.

The three men spent the next week sightseeing around Liverpool. Slowly Ben got his land legs back, and the ground beneath his feet stopped feeling like it was swaying. During this time, Ben wrote to Benjamin Franklin, who served as Pennsylvania's agent in London. Franklin was the most famous American colonist in Great Britain, and Ben hoped the older man would write him a letter of recommendation to the professors at Edinburgh University.

Ben, Johnathan, and James expected they would all travel north to Scotland together. But on the last day of their sightseeing in Liverpool, James felt ill and returned early to their rented room. That night, Ben and Johnathan were awakened by groaning. It was James. Ben lit several candles, and the two young men rushed to James's side. James was convulsing. Ben grabbed his medical bag, took out a lancet, and sliced across the vein in James's forearm. The two young doctors worked hard, and the convulsions stopped, but it was obvious to the two of them that James was gravely ill. In the morning, they called for a local doctor to come and examine their companion. However, the three medical men could not save James, who died that night.

Ben and Johnathan found themselves arranging a burial for their friend. An Anglican vicar sold them a plot in the local churchyard, where they buried James. It was a sobering reminder to Ben of how, despite the best medical care, a life could be lost in a matter of days.

Leaving James buried in a church graveyard in Liverpool, Ben and Johnathan climbed into a stagecoach bound for Edinburgh, Scotland. It was late fall, and the ground was soggy from the rain, making the track difficult for the horses to navigate. On the first night of the journey the travelers stayed at a tavern. The next day their progress was stopped by a flooded stream, and the stagecoach passengers sought shelter for the night in a nearby mud-brick home. The place consisted of a single room with a few rickety pieces of furniture. The couple who lived in the mud house shared their dinner—a bowl of milk—with the men.

Ben and Johnathan slept in their fur coats, hoping to create a barrier between them and the lice and fleas that inhabited the bed they were given to sleep on. Despite their best efforts, the next morning they were covered in bites and itched as they climbed back into the stagecoach.

As they traveled north, the huts got smaller. Ben could see that the single rooms were inhabited not only by farmers and their families, but also by hogs, horses, and cows. In Philadelphia he'd heard about how poor many of those living in the British countryside were. Now he was seeing the true depth of their poverty with his own eyes.

Despite the obvious poverty, Ben saw things throughout the countryside that delighted him. He caught glimpses of tree-lined lakes and the arches and walls of crumbling castles. The coach driver said that some of the ruins were over a thousand years old. Ben had learned British history in school, but now it was coming alive for him.

After four harrowing days in a springless stage-coach, Ben spied the unmistakable outline of Edinburgh Castle high atop Castle Rock. He had made it to his destination.

Ben and Johnathan spent their first night in Edinburgh at an inn. They then asked around until they found two unmarried older sisters who provided room and board to students. The rooms were on the fourth floor of a ten-story building. Ben had never seen a building that tall before, let alone gone inside one. Edinburgh had so many tall buildings that walking down a back alley was like passing through a canyon.

It was hard to believe that eighty thousand people—more than twice the population of Philadelphia—were crammed into the compact space that Edinburgh occupied. It was even harder to believe that few of the homes had outdoor privies. Instead, at ten o'clock in the evening, when everyone had gone home, people threw their day's toilet waste out the windows. The waste landed in the cobblestone street and mixed with horse dung. Each evening a "night soil man" shoveled the stinking piles of waste into a cart and hauled it away. But the city streets never properly got clean until a deluge of rain washed away the sludge. Ben was shocked by this. Until recently, Philadelphia had had a problem with stinking garbage and waste matter collecting in streams and stagnant ponds. The city had followed plans drawn up by Benjamin Franklin and had created sewers and storm drains. Ben hoped it wouldn't be long before Edinburgh figured out how to do the same.

Once Ben adjusted to his new surroundings, he took the letters of introduction he'd carried with him from Pennsylvania and set out with Johnathan to enroll at the University of Edinburgh. The university was nearly two hundred years old. It was also the top university of science and medicine in the world. Ben was surprised to discover that despite its prestige, the institution was housed in what looked like rows of horse stables. The University of Edinburgh had no permanent buildings of its own, and the students met together in an array of rented rooms.

At the university, Ben and Johnathan first called on Dr. William Cullen. The doctor's eyes lit up when he heard their names. "Ah," he said, in his Scottish brogue. "I have already received a letter of recommendation from Dr. Franklin."

"I am pleased to hear that," Ben replied, relieved that Benjamin Franklin had followed up on Ben's request so quickly. "And I have another letter of recommendation from Dr. John Morgan in Philadelphia," Ben added.

Ben handed Dr. Cullen the letter. When the doctor had read it, he laid it down and smiled. "I have many students and many obligations outside of the university," he told Ben and Johnathan. "But however close my attention may be to these necessary tasks, young gentlemen recommended to me by Dr. Morgan may always depend upon my immediate patronage and friendship. Please feel free to call upon me with any requests you have."

Ben was delighted. He knew that university life would go much more smoothly with the friendship of a powerful professor.

The next step in the process of enrolling was for Ben to buy tickets for the classes he wanted to take. Then it was off to visit the provost. Ben and Johnathan sat in the provost's office as he read them a list of student rules, which they had to promise to obey. The rules included respecting all professors, refraining from participating in riots, and working hard at their studies. Ben took up a quill pen, dipped it in ink, and signed the matriculation book. He was now officially a student of Edinburgh University.

Ben purchased several leather-bound blank books in which to keep his lecture notes. Since there were no textbooks for his classes, everything he wanted to remember from a lecture needed to be carefully recorded in one of his notebooks. Some of the students had learned shorthand before arriving. Ben wished he had too. After a lecture, those who didn't know shorthand gathered to read over their notes together, hoping to catch anything they might have missed. Most of the lecturers spoke in Latin, which, combined with their strong Scottish accents, made it difficult for Ben to understand and take notes.

Lectures were held six days a week, with Sunday off to attend church. Ben soon fell into a routine.

He got up at seven and studied in his room through the morning. At noon he went to classes and then followed doctors around the wards of the royal infirmary, listening to the doctors assess and recommend treatments for patients. After supper at 6:00 p.m., long after the sun had gone down, Ben settled into his room to copy out his notes and read. He blew his candle out at midnight and went to bed, to be awakened the next morning by the chiming bells of St. Giles.

It didn't take Ben long to realize that some of his lecturers were better than others. Dr. John Hope was particularly frustrating. He spoke in a low voice and often rambled on about religion instead of talking about the various botany topics he was supposed to cover. Dr. Joseph Black, the chemistry professor, was much more straightforward. He was a renowned scientist, and Ben loved the engaging way he used experiments to illustrate his lectures.

William Cullen soon became Ben's favorite lecturer. For one, he lectured in English, which Ben appreciated. Dr. Cullen lectured about diseases and in particular nosology, or the classifying of diseases into classes, orders, genera, and species. It was similar to Carl Linnaeus's attempts in botany to classify plants. Dr. Cullen also lectured about how he believed life emanated from the energy within the brain, which then passed through the nerves to the organs and muscles. Ben took detailed notes on all that William Cullen said.

Before long Ben became friends with a number of fellow students. They came from Scotland, England,

Ireland, the American colonies, the West Indies, Portugal, Italy, France, Holland, Germany, Switzerland, Russia, and Denmark to learn the latest in medical theory and practice.

Ben also received a constant stream of letters from home, replying to each of them. In one reply he commented on the Scottish game of golf. After playing it with friends, he described it as "a large common, in which there are several little holes, that is chosen for the purpose. It is played with little leather balls stuffed with feathers and with sticks made somewhat in the form of a bandy-wicket. He who puts the ball into a given number of holes, with the fewest strokes, gets the game."

Ben's brother Jacob wrote to him about the effects of the Townshend Acts passed by the British Parliament in 1767. Like the repealed Stamp Act, these acts were another attempt by Parliament to collect revenue from the American colonists by putting customs duties on imports of glass, lead, paint, paper, and tea. Jacob explained that the colonists were outraged, and as with the Stamp Act, were planning a boycott by agreeing not to import anything from England. Ben wondered where the meddling of the British Parliament in the affairs of the American colonies would end.

After just a few months at Edinburgh University, Johnathan returned home to Philadelphia. Grace Richardson, his fiancée, was ill, and he felt he needed to be with her. Ben was sad to see Johnathan go, though by now he felt at home in Edinburgh. His friends often invited him to stay at country homes for the weekend or to dine with Edinburgh's richest and most interesting people. He enjoyed every moment of such visits, often talking late into the evening with his hosts.

Chapter 6

Interesting and Important People

In February 1767, Ben received a visit from Richard Stockton, a wealthy Philadelphia lawyer. Richard was on the board of trustees for the College of New Jersey and had also been a friend of Samuel Finley, Ben's uncle and the past president of the college. Richard explained to Ben that the board of trustees had sent him to Scotland to inform the Reverend John Witherspoon that he'd been chosen as the next president of the College of New Jersey. Ben was delighted with the news. John Witherspoon was a revered theologian and would make a perfect president for the college.

Ben enjoyed Richard's visit, especially talking with him about Philadelphia, his Uncle Samuel, and the future of the College of New Jersey. From

Edinburgh, Richard headed south to Paisley, near Glasgow, where John Witherspoon lived. Not too long afterward, Ben received a letter from Richard informing him that while John was honored to be chosen for the president's position, his wife refused to go with him, saying she was terrified of the sea voyage to America. And so John had turned down the position.

It was hard for Ben to believe. John Witherspoon was the perfect choice for president of the College of New Jersey. While Richard headed back to North America Ben sprang into action. He began a correspondence with John and was soon invited to spend a weekend with the Witherspoons at their home in Paisley. During that weekend, despite his own terrible experience crossing the Atlantic Ocean by ship, Ben managed to calm Mrs. Witherspoon's fear of the voyage. Mrs. Witherspoon finally agreed to the journey so that her husband could accept the position of president of the College of New Jersey. Ben was delighted with the outcome.

Two years of study at the University of Edinburgh sped by, and on June 19, 1768, Ben was awarded his Doctor of Medicine degree. For his thesis, he'd focused on digestion in the stomach, trying to give a chemical explanation for it. In the process of his research, Ben had conducted four experiments, three on himself and one on a friend. The experiments involved eating a number of different foods, waiting two to three hours while the foods processed in the stomach, and then vomiting up the recently eaten food and analyzing it, testing to see if the food had absorbed acid or was fermenting. Following the experiments and analysis, Ben wrote his thesis in English, then translated it into Latin for submission.

Having earned his degree, Ben wrote home to his mother and stepfather, seeking their permission to extend his stay in Great Britain. He wanted to see firsthand the latest medical techniques being employed in London. While he waited to hear back, Ben spent a relaxing summer with his friends the Leslie family at Melville House, their country estate in Fifeshire, north of Edinburgh. There he enjoyed participating in the family's lively and witty conversation and taking long walks through the heather. At the end of summer Ben received a letter from Philadelphia giving him permission to extend his stay.

In September 1768 Ben set out set out on the eleven-day stagecoach journey to London. The horses clopped along at a steady four miles per hour through the green countryside and the villages of Tottenham, Islington, and Pentonville. As they got closer to the city, the roads became crowded with carts, riders on horseback, beggars, and farmers taking their produce into the city to sell. As he entered London, Ben was astonished by the noise and activity on the cobbled streets, the pall of black smoke that hung over the city, and the soot and grime that seemed to settle on everything.

In London, Ben's second cousin, Thomas Coombe, was studying to become an Anglican clergyman. He was living in a boardinghouse on Haymarket and invited Ben to stay with him. This suited Ben. The location was close to London's three main hospitals: Middlesex, St. Thomas', and Guy's.

It didn't take Ben long to realize that London was a lot different from Edinburgh. It had twice the population of Edinburgh and sprawled along the banks of the River Thames. But the distinctions ran deeper. Edinburgh was full of staid Presbyterians who studied more than they drank. London was a glittering capital, the largest city in Europe, replete with coffeehouses, private clubs, beautiful church buildings, and, of course, Parliament. The city also had its dark side. It was dirty, the living conditions for many were cramped and unhealthy, and there seemed to be drunken men, women, and children on every street corner. Gin seemed to be for sale everywhere. The city was also crime ridden, even though more than two hundred offenses, including petty theft, were punishable by death.

After settling into the boardinghouse with his cousin Thomas, Ben visited Benjamin Franklin. Ben found Benjamin Franklin to still be sprightly, even though at sixty-two years of age he was old enough to be Ben's grandfather. Benjamin Franklin had lived in London for nearly four years, serving as the Pennsylvania Assembly's representative. The two men took an immediate liking to each other, and Benjamin Franklin introduced Ben to a number of the most interesting and important people in London. One of these was Dr. John Fothergill, a Quaker and a celebrated London doctor.

Dr. Fothergill took Ben to see his personal botanical garden. Ben was amazed at the variety of medicinal plants the doctor grew in a huge glasshouse and on the grounds surrounding his home near Stratford. Every plant and tree seemed to have a story, and Dr. Fothergill delighted in telling Ben about each one. Among the plants were a type of magnolia bush from the Straits of Magellan on the tip of South America, rhubarb from Russia, a cinchona tree from Peru whose bark was a source of quinine, and beautiful red opium poppies from Turkey.

John Fothergill was one of the busiest men Ben had ever met. He seemed to do so many things besides running a bustling medical practice. He told Ben that he was trying to work out the relationship between the weather and human diseases. For several years, each day he'd recorded the temperature, air pressure, wind direction, rain levels, and fog density or sunshine intensity to understand what diseases peaked with different weather conditions. He urged Ben to do the same when he returned to Philadelphia.

Through Dr. Fothergill, Ben met another Quaker physician, John Lettsom. At twenty-four years of age, John Lettsom was two years older than Ben. Though the two men came from very different backgrounds, they got along well. John had been born on the island of Little Jost Van Dyke in the Virgin Islands. His father owned cotton and sugar plantations on which he kept about fifty slaves to do most of the work. When John was six years old, he had been sent to live with a Quaker family in Lancaster,

England, to be educated. Like Ben, John had served his apprenticeship to qualify as a doctor and was now pursing an advanced degree in medicine.

John Lettsom told Ben how, on learning of the death of his father the year before, he had interrupted his studies and returned to the Virgin Islands to settle his father's estate. One of the things John had done while settling the estate stunned Ben. The plantation slaves John's father had owned were worth 450 pounds each if sold—a small fortune. However, John explained to Ben that instead of selling the slaves, he had given them their freedom.

Ben had been familiar with the sight of slaves in Philadelphia. When his father died, his mother had sold most of the family's slaves, retaining only one to work at the Blazing Star. However, Ben had never heard of a master setting his slaves free. Yet that was exactly what John had done, letting a fortune slip through his fingers in the process. While Ben had come to London to learn about medicine, he realized his English physician friends were teaching him much more—such as the notion that slaves could be set free to live and work like other people.

Ben's medical degree from Edinburgh University allowed him to buy tickets to "walk the wards" with London's best doctors. He paid twenty guineas to follow Dr. Richard Huck around the wards of St. Thomas' Hospital. Dr. Huck, the royal physician, had served as an army physician in the West Indies during the recent French and Indian War. As a result, he had a soft spot for American colonists, though he made certain that Ben knew he was an unapologetic supporter of the British monarchy. Ben followed Dr. Huck around St. Thomas' Hospital, taking notes as the doctor diagnosed and prescribed various treatments for patients. As had been the case during Ben's apprenticeship with Dr. Redman back in Philadelphia, these treatments normally involved a combination of cupping, bleeding, and purging.

By November it was cool enough for the most anticipated medical spectacle in London: the Hunter brothers' Dissection Demonstrations and Lectures held at the School of Anatomy located in their home on Great Windmill Street. These classes were carried out only in the fall and winter to allow dead bodies to last a week before they became too decomposed to dissect.

The Hunter brothers were originally from Scotland. The older brother, William, had been to medical school, while younger brother, John, served as his apprentice. The pair used the Paris method of teaching. Each student was given a cadaver to dissect, which they did under the precise instructions of John Hunter.

The course began with several lectures by William. The lectures held Ben spellbound, and before he knew it, the two hours allotted for each lecture had sped by. After attending the opening lectures, Ben arrived at the Hunter brothers' School of Anatomy to find cadavers laid out on tables, ready for dissection. As Ben looked at all the bodies, his mind went back to Philadelphia. He recalled the dissection that William Shippen Jr., who'd also studied under the Hunter brothers, had carried out in the small laboratory building behind his father's house. He also remembered the riot that had occurred.

Somehow, in London, the Hunter brothers seemed to have an endless supply of cadavers to dissect. Ben soon learned that John Hunter bought the dead bodies from grave robbers—or Resurrectionists, as they called themselves. John sometimes also dug up freshly buried bodies himself or arranged for them to be smuggled out of hospitals. John not only dissected human bodies, but also collected animals—dead and alive. When Ben visited John's country estate two miles outside London, he was astonished to see zebras, lions, leopards, and Asian buffaloes on the grounds, while inside the house was an amazing array of varnished animal bones, dried skins, and preserved organs.

While he learned about the newest medical practices by day, in the evenings Ben attended dinner parties with all sorts of interesting and informed people. The causes and cures of social problems were discussed at these events. In London, with its large and growing population, poor people often lived in cellars and tenements, which were usually damp, drafty, and rat infested. And those who could not afford even such substandard accommodations were forced to live and fend for themselves on the streets. At one dinner party, Benjamin Franklin told Ben that London had a particularly high death rate, especially among young children. Approximately twenty-one children of every hundred born alive died before they were two years old. Most of these deaths were caused by substandard living conditions and poor hygiene practices.

In these discussions Ben also learned that the poor were taken advantage of. One dinner party guest explained that poor laborers and artisans often received their wages in alehouses on Saturday nights. However, the alehouse owners would tip the paymasters if they waited until late in the evening before arriving to pay the workers. While the laborers waited for their wages, they would consume mug after mug of alcohol. By the time the paymasters did arrive, most of the laborers' wages would go to cover the cost of the alcohol. Such practices simply kept the poor locked in their poverty. During such dinner conversations, Ben realized that while there were many ideas about the causes of London's social problems, little was being done to solve them.

During his time in London, Ben also spent many hours in coffee shops discussing the situation in North America. British newspapers were filled with the latest news from the American colonies. Like many others, Ben was shocked to read that on October 1, 1768, the British had ordered four regiments from Halifax, Nova Scotia, to occupy Boston. This was because of the Liberty Affair. The *Liberty* was a merchant ship belonging to Boston importer John Hancock. It had anchored in Boston Harbor, and two tidesmen had boarded her. Tidesmen were men charged with not allowing anyone or anything on or off the ship until it had passed through customs. The following morning, when customs officers boarded the ship, only a quarter of the ship's hold was filled with casks of Madeira wine. The rest of the hold space was empty. The customs officers accused John Hancock of unloading most of his cargo under cover of darkness, though the tidesmen insisted they had seen nothing.

Several weeks later, one of the tidesmen claimed that he'd been tied up and had his life threatened if he told anyone that the *Liberty*'s cargo had been unloaded during the night. The customs office in Boston then seized the ship, after which riots broke out. Lord Hillsborough, secretary of state for the colonies, had ordered the four regiments of troops to occupy Boston and quell the uprising. Benjamin Franklin told Ben that he thought that sending troops into Boston was a dangerous step for the British to take. It seemed to him like setting up a blacksmith's forge in a magazine of gunpowder. Sooner or later a spark was going to cause the gunpowder to explode.

More than the Liberty Affair, however, it seemed to Ben that everyone he knew in London wanted to discuss a pamphlet titled *Letters from a Farmer in Pennsylvania to the Inhabitants of the British Colonies* by John Dickinson. Ben had met John during his medical apprenticeship. Far from being a farmer, John Dickinson was a well-off Philadelphia lawyer. He had written a series of twelve letters to the editor of the *Pennsylvania Chronicle and Universal Advertiser.* The letters were quickly reprinted in newspapers throughout the colonies. They were also bound together into pamphlet form and sold in Philadelphia, Boston, New York, London, Paris, and Dublin.

The twelve letters contained in the pamphlet railed against the Townshend Acts. The main purpose of the acts was to raise revenue in the American colonies to pay the salaries of colonial governors and judges loyal to Great Britain. While John Dickinson acknowledged the power of Parliament in matters regarding the British Empire, he also argued that the colonies were sovereign in their internal affairs. Given this view, he asserted that any taxes Parliament put upon the colonies for the purpose of raising revenue were unconstitutional.

Even though Ben hadn't experienced life under the Townshend Acts, he knew firsthand the strife the Stamp Act had visited upon the American colonies. As a result, he found himself agreeing with John's assertions.

During his spare time in London, Ben took in the sights of the city. He especially enjoyed visiting the newly completed British Museum, along with Westminster Abbey, the Tower of London, and the Houses of Parliament. All the while he jotted down copious notes in his commonplace book, journaled, and wrote letters to friends and family back in Pennsylvania. After visiting the Houses of Parliament, he wrote to his school friend Ebenezer Hazard.

> I went a few days ago in company with a Danish physician to visit the House of Lords and the House of Commons. When I went into the first, I felt as if I walked on sacred ground. I gazed for some time at the Throne with emotions that I cannot describe. I asked

our guide if it was common for strangers to set down upon it. He told me no, but upon my importuning him a good deal I prevailed upon him to allow me the liberty. I accordingly advanced toward it and sat in it for a considerable time. . . .

From this I went to the House of Commons. I cannot say I felt as if I walked on "sacred ground" here. This, I thought, is the place where the infernal scheme for enslaving America was first broached. Here the usurping Commons first endeavored to rob the King of his supremacy over the colonies and to divide it among themselves. O! cursed haunt of venality, bribery, and corruption! In the mist of these reflections I asked where Mr. Pitt . . . stood when he spoke in favor of repealing the Stamp Act. "Here," said our guide, "on this very spot." I then went up to it, sat down upon [the seat] for some time, and fancying myself surrounded with a crowded House, rose up from my seat and began to repeat part of his speech: "When the scheme for taxing America," said I, "was first proposed, I was unhappily confined to my bed. But had some kind hand brought me and laid me down upon *this* floor, I would have bore a public testimony against it. Americans are the sons, not the bastards of Englishmen. I rejoice that America has resisted."

Ben's five months in London flew by. He knew it would soon be time for him to return home to Philadelphia. But before leaving, Benjamin Franklin encouraged him to visit Paris, France. Since Ben was running short of funds, Benjamin Franklin even loaned him the money to go. In mid-February 1769, twenty-three-year-old Benjamin Rush crossed the English Channel to France.

Chapter 7

A Well-Trained Colonial Doctor

Upon his arrival in France, Ben was pleasantly surprised by the welcome he received. He hadn't been sure what to expect from the French, since he was from an American colony and the French and Indian War had ended six years before, with France losing. However, in Paris it seemed that Benjamin Franklin was well loved, and his letters of introduction carried a lot of weight.

Within days of reaching Paris, Ben was taken under the wing of Dr. Jacques Barbeu-Dubourg and was soon caught up in the whirl of Parisian intellectual circles. Dr. Barbeu-Dubourg was a physician and a botanist. He was also a great admirer of Benjamin Franklin and had translated several of his books into French. The doctor had ideas of his own about health and happily shared them with Ben. He had tried bathing in cold water, as Benjamin Franklin did, but found it too "violent." Instead, he sat naked for an hour each morning, "bathing" in the cold air.

Ben wasn't so impressed with this idea, but he was astonished when Dr. Barbeu-Dubourg showed him his *carte chronographique*, a machine the doctor had invented. The machine allowed a reader to scroll through a fifty-four-foot roll of paper on which was recorded all the important events in world history from the birth of Adam to the death of Pope Benedict XIV in 1758. Ben was intrigued by the ingeniousness of the carte chronographique. On the scroll the years were marked across the top, and 140 years could be displayed at a time. The column beneath each year recorded the various important historical events that had taken place. The carte chronographique had two wooden handles so the scroll could be rolled to the left or the right. Scrolling to the left took you forward through history toward the present, and scrolling right took you back through history. Ben passed several enjoyable hours scrolling back and forth through time.

Through Dr. Barbeu-Dubourg, Ben met some of the top surgeons and doctors in Paris. Ben hoped to learn from them, but what he saw of their work didn't impress him. The Hôtel Dieu, the oldest hospital in Paris, was so short of room that four patients had to share one bed. To make matters worse, the hospital's medical practices were fifty years out-of-date.

Ben also visited the Foundling Hospital. As in London, many babies in Paris were born to mothers who could not provide for them, and the Foundling Hospital tried to save as many of them as possible. Ben was shown a baby basket that was left at the hospital gate. Desperate new mothers knew that they could place their baby in the basket, ring the bell above it, and walk away. Someone from the hospital would hear the bell and retrieve the baby. Ben was shocked to learn that over six hundred babies were abandoned each month, and half of them died before they turned two years old. However, Ben did appreciate the motto from Psalm 27:10 inscribed over the hospital door: "Though my mother and father have abandoned me, yet the LORD will take me up."

Everywhere Ben went, it seemed, French men and women knew of the tension between the American colonies and the British Parliament. They asked him questions about it, which he tried his best to answer. He pointed out, however, that he'd been away from the colonies for two and a half years and didn't have much firsthand knowledge of the situation other than what he had been told in letters from home.

Visiting a predominantly Roman Catholic country for the first time caused Ben to think about his view of Protestantism. On the way back to London he stopped at the Roman Catholic monastery in Amiens, where he observed an old priest going about his prayers, chanting and lighting candles. That night Ben wrote in his journal,

> This holy Man (said I to myself) has betook himself this Morning, to this Sanctuary, in Order to offer up his Morning Oblations to

> Heaven. The flame of Devotion can burn notwithstanding it is kindled upon the altar of superstition. The Deity pays no Regard to those little Ceremonies, in worship which divide most of the Christian Churches. He will always worship acceptably, who worships him in Spirit and in Truth. The Perfume of flowers is the same in whosoever soil they grow.

Ben returned to London on March 21, 1769. The slow trip across the English Channel from Calais took twenty-three hours. Ben was glad to be on solid ground again when the ship reached Dover, England.

The coach trip from Dover back to London had its share of excitement. The coachman stopped to help a woman lying by the side of the road and discovered she was about to give birth. Ben rushed to help deliver the baby. In gratitude, the mother named her new son Benjamin Rush.

Ben was still feeling good about helping little Benjamin Rush as he prepared to sail home to Philadelphia. It was time for him to move on to the next stage of his life, that of being a well-trained colonial doctor.

Before leaving England, Ben was introduced to Thomas Penn, son of William Penn and the current proprietor of Pennsylvania. Thomas presented Ben with the latest chemical apparatus for use in the new medical school at the College of Philadelphia. Ben carefully packed the equipment in sawdust inside wooden chests to protect it from damage on the voyage. He looked forward to getting home. If things worked out the way he hoped, and as letters from John Morgan and William Shippen Jr. hinted, he might well be appointed professor of chemistry at the medical college.

Ben sailed for North America aboard the *Edward*. He departed from Gravesend, near the mouth of the River Thames, on May 26, 1769. As he sailed away, Ben wondered if he would ever see Great Britain again.

The voyage across the Atlantic lasted forty-nine days. This time the weather was mostly calm, allowing Ben plenty of time to study without feeling seasick. At the end of the voyage, the *Edward* anchored off the Battery at the tip of Manhattan Island in New York. Ben's friend Ebenezer Hazard was waiting on the dock to meet Ben when he was rowed ashore. After greeting each other, the two men walked up Broad Street to a teahouse. Ben ordered bread and butter and declared it to be the best meal he'd eaten in a long while.

The following day Ben loaded himself and his baggage onto a stagecoach for the trip back to Philadelphia. His brother Jacob rode out to meet him at Bristol, Pennsylvania, and the two brothers traveled the last twenty miles to Philadelphia together. Ben remembered his younger brother as a gangly eighteen-year-old. Now Jacob was twenty-one and had just earned his Doctor of Law degree at the College of New Jersey and had been admitted to the Philadelphia Bar. Ben congratulated him on his achievement.

The three years away had brought other changes at home. Both of his sisters were now widows and had three small children to raise. Ben knew that he would be expected to help his sisters financially.

Within weeks, Ben, Jacob, and their sister Rebecca Stamper moved in to a home on Arch Street. Rebecca agreed to be the housekeeper for her two brothers.

At twenty-three years of age, with a medical degree from the top university in the world, Ben set out to make a name and a following for himself in Philadelphia. He set up a medical practice, and on August 1, 1769, he saw his first patient, a woman named Lydia Hyde. On the same day, the board of the College of Philadelphia chose Ben to become its chemistry professor at the medical school. This was a great honor, since it was the first professorship of its kind in any of the American colonies. Four other men were on the faculty of the medical school. John Morgan was professor of the theory and practice of medicine; William Shippen Jr. was professor of anatomy, surgery, and midwifery; Adam Kuhn was professor of botany and *materia medica*; and Thomas Bond, the cofounder of Pennsylvania Hospital, was professor of clinical medicine.

Although Ben was five years younger than Adam Kuhn and thirty-five years younger than Thomas Bond, he felt confident that he could fit in to the faculty. He had detailed notes from Dr. Joseph Black, his chemistry professor in Edinburgh, and intended to make some changes to them before the school opened on November 1.

Ben's chemistry lectures closely followed the structure of Dr. Black's course. Ben discussed a range of topics and used experiments to illustrate the points he was trying to make. He dropped a marble into a beaker of sulfuric acid, and his students watched as the marble dissolved. He poured oil on top of water in another beaker and showed his students how the two liquids did not mix. He shook the beaker and the liquids mixed, then separated again. Ben asked his students to hypothesize about what was happening. Ben told his students that most scientists, including himself, believed that a mineral existed somewhere on earth that could cure every disease of the human body.

During the fall, as Ben taught chemistry and attended to his medical practice, he, Jacob, and Rebecca moved to another home on the corner of Front and Walnut Streets. From the upstairs windows Ben had a great view of the Delaware River docks, bustling with ships unloading tobacco, cotton, spices, and slaves from the southern colonies and the West Indies. Ben was amazed by how busy Philadelphia had become while he was away in Great Britain. It was now the third largest city in the British Empire after London and Edinburgh, expanding rapidly to the north and south along the banks of the Delaware River.

Ben's medical practice grew slowly from just seven paying patients in his first month to twenty per month by Christmas. In fact, he saw many more than that. Most of Ben's first patients were poor, and he charged only those who could afford to pay for his services. Some mornings he saw sixteen or more patients, and only one of them would pay him.

In the afternoons, when he was not teaching, Ben made his doctor's rounds, visiting sick people in their homes. He soon grew used to climbing rickety ladders into lofts where poor families huddled without a stove or blankets. Most of them hadn't had a bath in ten years or more. After some visits, Ben would be covered with lice and fleas, but he never hesitated to help alleviate the suffering of the poor and needy. Since he was unable to afford his own carriage or sedan chair, he walked to most of his appointments or rode a horse if he was called out into the countryside.

When he wasn't giving chemistry lectures or seeing patients, Ben wrote opinion pieces for newspapers and articles for the American Philosophy Society, of which he had just become a founding member. He also wrote educational booklets for the public on diet, exercise, and digestion. Some of the ideas he put forward in these booklets were eagerly received, such as his encouragement to walk, run, and dance. Other ideas, such as eating just one meal a day in the evening, were viewed with suspicion.

All the while, Ben kept up-to-date with the swiftly changing political situation in the colonies. Most of the unrest seemed to be centered in Boston, Massachusetts. This made sense to Ben, since British troops were occupying the city. On March 5, 1770, resentment on the part of colonists and frustration on the part of British soldiers turned violent. Three days later, Ben read in the newspaper of a clash between the soldiers and a local mob that left four colonists dead and one fighting for his life. The anti-British colonists soon dubbed it The Boston Massacre, while the British called it The Incident on King Street. Ben was sure that it would turn out to be more than just an incident.

That summer an epidemic of scarlet fever broke out among the children of Philadelphia. Ben treated the sick children as best he could and took detailed notes on how they responded to his medicines. Sadly, despite the medicine, many of the children with the disease died.

In the fall, Jacob left Philadelphia to study law in London. Ben sent a satchel of letters of introduction with him. He was proud that his brother was heading off to England, but it did add to his financial pressure. Ben now had to make enough money to send cash to Jacob in England while still supporting himself and his sister.

To earn more money, Ben took on seven apprentices to help expand his medical practice and see more patients. He soon realized he'd been too ambitious. The young apprentices were hard to handle as a group. They lived in the house with him and his sister Rebecca, but they were loud and exhausting to be around. Ben knew he couldn't keep up his busy study schedule with so many young men in the noisy house. He rented a nearby loft in which he installed bunk beds, and the seven apprentices moved in. They lived close enough for Ben to keep his eye on them but far enough away to be out of earshot.

Once Ben had his apprentices under control, the following year passed quickly for him. He saw patients and wrote the first chemistry textbook in America, along with hundreds of letters and notes in his commonplace book and journals. He seldom went out at night, preferring to read or study.

Ben's biggest challenge was dealing with the rest of the medical school faculty. Ben had remained an enthusiastic follower of the theories put forward by his professor at Edinburgh University, Dr. William Cullen. However, the other four medical school faculty members were not so keen on Dr. Cullen's notions about classifying diseases and where life emanated from in the body. When Ben passed on Dr. Cullen's ideas to his students, Ben clashed with John Morgan and particularly William Shippen Jr. Ben suspected Dr. Shippen was actively discouraging students from attending his chemistry lectures. Despite the tension among the medical school faculty, Ben continued his work lecturing, seeing patients, and keeping meticulous notes on patients' symptoms and treatments.

During summer 1773, Philadelphia was struck with a smallpox epidemic, and Ben sprang into action, treating those who contracted the disease. He also joined with a group of doctors to help inoculate children against the disease for free. The first step was to induce vomiting and diarrhea to clean out a patient's system. Then the doctor made a cut on the person's arm and filled it with pus from the sore of someone who had the disease. The arm was bandaged, and the patient waited for a rash to develop. Once this happened, the patient suffered from a slightly milder form of smallpox that lasted four to six weeks. All the while the patient remained isolated and under the care of a doctor until he or she got well. Once patients had recovered, they had a very low chance of ever catching smallpox again.

While studying in Great Britain, Ben had learned of the Suttonian method for inoculation. This approach focused on using diet and medicinal wines to prepare people for inoculation and sustain them through the disease period. Also, instead of using a cut in which to introduce the smallpox matter, the Suttonian method used a pinprick on the arm. Ben used the Suttonian method when he inoculated children during the smallpox outbreak. The approach made him very popular as a physician, since it seemed far less barbaric to most people. Of course, the new inoculation approach also brought Ben into conflict with some of the older doctors in town who believed that the traditional way was the best.

When the smallpox epidemic in Philadelphia subsided, three hundred people had died from the disease, but a great number of young people who had been inoculated had survived.

During 1773 Ben wrote another pamphlet, this time on an explosive topic that had nothing to do with medicine. He titled the pamphlet *An Address to the Inhabitants of the British Settlement in America upon Slave-Keeping.* For some time Ben had been thinking about the morality of owning slaves. He'd been appalled to see so many slave ships in Liverpool Harbor when he arrived in England. He also remembered the view that Samuel Davies had shared with him and the other students at the College of New

Jersey, that a black slave was just as intelligent as his or her white slave owner. Ben had also been challenged by how John Lettsom had freed the slaves he inherited from his father in the Virgin Islands and by the discussions about slavery that the two men had had in London.

Since returning home to Philadelphia, Ben had spent many afternoons meeting important people at the England Coffeehouse. While the coffeehouse had strict rules against playing cards or swearing, it hosted the auction and sale of slaves from the Caribbean and the Gold Coast of Africa when slave ships arrived in Philadelphia. Each slave was made to stand atop a barrel by the door as the auctioneer described him or her according to age, health, strength, and, in the case of girls and women, the likelihood of their bearing children for their new master. This was part of life for many colonists in North America, and at first it had not bothered Ben. But as he considered what it meant to be a slave, Ben concluded that it must be a terrible life to be bought and sold like livestock, not knowing who would buy you or what you would be forced to do.

Ben's ideas turned to action. Although it took him weeks of working long into the night, he managed to write down exactly what he thought of slavery in America. He wrote about the terrible lives many slaves lived and about how wrong it was to use the Bible to justify slavery. He also urged that the importation of slaves be banned completely and that those who were already in the colonies be freed.

In late 1773, *An Address to the Inhabitants of the British Settlement in America upon Slave-Keeping* was published. Simultaneously, a petition to the Pennsylvania Assembly urged a tax increase on imported slaves to reduce the number of slaves being brought into the colony. Although the petition was not what Ben advocated in his publication, it was a start. Ben knew that by publishing the pamphlet, he was straying away from his medical writing and into politics. He also was aware that it would probably cost him some of his wealthy patients, but he didn't care. He had to raise his voice on the issue.

Chapter 8

The Point of No Return

On December 18, 1773, Ben read a local newspaper report of an event that was being dubbed the Boston Tea Party. On the evening of December 16, about fifty colonists disguised as Indians stormed Griffin's Wharf in Boston. Three East India Company ships, the *Dartmouth*, *Eleanor*, and *Beaver*, each carrying tea, were docked there. The colonists seized control of the ships and dumped a total of 340 heavy chests of tea, worth nine thousand British pounds, into Boston Harbor.

When the unpopular Townshend Acts had been repealed in 1770, members of Parliament in London left in place one tax: a tax on tea. This tax was enshrined in the Tea Act, which was passed by Parliament and signed into law on May 10, 1773. While the American colonists had become accustomed to paying a tax on tea, the Tea Act also gave the East India Company the exclusive right to ship and sell tea in North America. This meant that merchants could no longer purchase cheaper tea overseas and import it into the colonies. Instead they had to buy their tea solely from the East India Company, which operated under a royal charter. It was frustration with this situation that led to the ransacking of the three ships and the dumping of tea into Boston Harbor.

Following the Boston Tea Party, Ben, like many other colonists, waited to see what would happen next. It didn't take long to find out. In March 1774, the British Parliament passed the Boston Port Act that completely closed Boston Harbor to all ships. Under the act the Boston customs house was to be relocated south to Plymouth, and the seat of Massachusetts colonial government was ordered to move to the city of Salem. By May 1774, the other American colonies were sending aid to Boston.

Until now, each colony in North America had had its own laws and relationship with Great Britain. But given the treatment of Massachusetts by Parliament and King George III, Massachusetts leaders sent a letter to each of the thirteen colonies, asking them to stop all trade with Great Britain. Ben thought this was a great idea. It was time to show Parliament that the American colonies could not be bullied. However, many others in Philadelphia did not share Ben's view. These people did not want to meddle in another colony's affairs. The Quakers were included in this group, and they did not want to do anything that might hint of eventual armed rebellion in the colonies against the British.

By June 1774 an extraordinary idea was taking shape. All the colonies except Georgia agreed to send delegates to a large meeting, or congress. There they would discuss their common concerns about the British and what action, if any, they should take. The Georgia colony had decided not to send delegates because white settlers there were having conflicts with the local Indians and they needed the British army to help subdue them.

Ben was delighted when he learned that the first Continental Congress would be held in Philadelphia. Although his medical practice was busier than ever, he relished the thought of some of the brightest people from the American colonies coming to his city. In fact, he was so excited that on August 29, 1774, he rode out to meet some of the arriving New England delegates. He encountered the coach carrying John Adams and Robert Treat Paine of Massachusetts. The two New Englanders immediately began peppering Ben with questions about what the Pennsylvania delegates thought Massachusetts should do next. Ben enjoyed their conversation so much that he invited John Adams to stay at his house for the first week of the gathering. When John Adams told Ben that his cousin Samuel Adams was traveling to the congress in another coach, Ben invited him to stay as well.

Although Ben wasn't a delegate to the Continental Congress himself, having John and Samuel Adams staying with him meant that he kept up-to-date on the discussions. After a week with Ben, John and Samuel Adams moved into Mrs. Yard's boardinghouse, though Ben visited them often to keep up with events.

The fifty-six delegates to the Continental Congress met for seven weeks at Carpenter's Hall in Philadelphia. During that time, Ben met all the delegates and got to know many of them well. He invited George Washington, a planter from Mount Vernon, Virginia, to dinner at his house. The two discussed how to make King George III understand how serious they were about demanding change in the American colonies.

At the end of the seven weeks, the Continental Congress delegates narrowly passed a vote to form an association of colonies that would agree not to import goods from or export goods to Great Britain. The congress also agreed to no longer import slaves from anywhere into the colonies after December 1, 1774. Ben was particularly happy about this. The congressional delegates also sent a letter to Parliament demanding Boston's liberation and asking that all American colonists receive the basic rights of English citizens. Ben was hopeful that the king and Parliament would understand the colonists' position and find a way to work with them. However, he thought it would probably take two or even three years for the king and Parliament to accept the colonists' demands.

In the meantime, the situation with Great Britain remained tense. Given the Continental Congress's ban on the import or export of goods from or to Great Britain, many believed it was only a matter of time before British navy ships began blockading American ports. If this were to happen, the colonists desperately needed several items to defend themselves. At the top of the list was saltpeter to make gunpowder. Until now this had been imported from the East India Company, but since the company was owned by the British, the colonists were sure that the saltpeter supply would be cut off. Ben set to work with several other men devising a way to use home-grown ingredients—tobacco stalks and cow dung mixed with animal and human urine—to make the white saltpeter crystals the colonies would need if they were to stand up to the British. Ben also wrote a booklet on the best ways to make saltpeter and then turned his attention to other things the colonists would need to either make or do without.

In February 1775, the United Company for Promoting American Manufacturers elected Benjamin Rush as their president. Until this time most manufactured items the American colonists needed were imported from England. Now, with the threat of this source being cut off, Americans had to find ways to manufacture their own goods, including cotton, woolen fabric, and linen for clothing.

Ben talked to as many people as he could about this situation. He learned that in Philadelphia alone, 250,000 pounds went to England each year to pay for British-made cloth. If the colonists could learn to make their own cloth in America, all that money could be kept at home and new jobs would be created. Ben put it this way: "A people who are entirely dependent upon foreigners for food or clothes must always be subject to them." He aimed to do whatever he could to help American colonists become self-sufficient until Great Britain changed its mind regarding the colonies.

Meanwhile, the British government decided that the colonies were in open rebellion and needed to be taught a firm lesson. King George III ordered colonial governors to shut down their legislatures and forbade anyone to attend a second Continental Congress. Almost every day the *Pennsylvania Journal* newspaper wrote about what people thought should happen next. Some colonists wanted to wait for the king or Parliament to announce a compromise, while others formed military-style groups—militias—that stockpiled weapons and trained men to fight.

The *Pennsylvania Journal* also reported on how other colonies were responding to the challenge from Great Britain. On March 23, 1775, Patrick Henry gave a fiery speech to the second Virginia Convention. The text of the speech was printed in the newspaper. Ben read it with interest, especially since he had met Patrick Henry at the first Continental Congress. The speech ended with Patrick Henry declaring,

> There is a just God who presides over the destinies of nations, and who will raise up friends to fight our battles for us. The battle, sir, is not to the strong alone; it is to the vigilant, the active, the brave. Besides, sir, we have no election. If we were base enough to desire it, it is now too late to retire from the contest.

> There is no retreat but in submission and slavery! Our chains are forged! Their clanking may be heard on the plains of Boston! The war is inevitable—and let it come! I repeat it, sir, let it come.
>
> It is in vain, sir, to extenuate the matter. Gentlemen may cry, Peace, Peace—but there is no peace. The war is actually begun! The next gale that sweeps from the north will bring to our ears the clash of resounding arms! Our brethren are already in the field! Why stand we here idle? What is it that gentlemen wish? What would they have? Is life so dear, or peace so sweet, as to be purchased at the price of chains and slavery? Forbid it, Almighty God! I know not what course others may take; but as for me, give me liberty or give me death!

After reading the text of the speech, Ben thought that Patrick Henry was too eager to go to war with the British. Given enough time, Ben believed a solution could be worked out.

That all changed on April 24, 1775, when news reached Philadelphia that on the evening of Tuesday, April 18, six hundred British soldiers had marched from Boston toward Lexington and Concord in Massachusetts. Their leader, Lieutenant Colonel Francis Smith, intended to confiscate the weapons and ammunition that local militia fighters had stored there and arrest Samuel Adams and John Hancock. However, word of the British advance reached the

Patriot militiamen. A volunteer band of militiamen gathered to confront the British. They fought hard at both Lexington and Concord, and after several small battles, the British troops retreated to Boston. Seventy-three British soldiers were killed in the fighting. By contrast, only forty-nine Patriot fighters were killed, and Samuel Adams and John Hancock both escaped capture.

Ben was appalled when he learned of the attack. Now he agreed with Patrick Henry: the time for compromise was over. The first shots of a revolution had been fired, and Ben wondered what would happen next.

Early the following month, Benjamin Franklin arrived back in Philadelphia. Ben was delighted to see him again, and the Pennsylvania Assembly unanimously chose Dr. Franklin as one of their delegates to the upcoming Second Continental Congress in Philadelphia.

On May 10, 1775, less than a week after Benjamin Franklin's return from England, the Second Continental Congress got under way. The delegates, who met this time in the Pennsylvania State House, were welcomed by the somber clanging of muffled church bells to commemorate the colonists killed by the British in Massachusetts. Once again, Ben was in the thick of things. He spent time at the local taverns and coffee shops, meeting with delegates and hearing their stories.

As he had been for the first Continental Congress, Peyton Randolph was elected president of the new congress. But two weeks in he was summoned back to Virginia. A young lawyer named Thomas Jefferson replaced Randolph in the Virginia delegation. Ben immediately liked Jefferson's frank, easy style.

John Adams and Ben were becoming good friends. John explained to Ben how he had left his home in Braintree, Massachusetts, and ridden through the battlefields. "The die is cast," he said. "We have crossed the point of no return."

George Washington was once again a member of the Virginia delegation, and he brought with him his old army uniform from his days fighting in the French and Indian War. Soon he was given the title of commander in chief of the American armies.

On May 27, 1775, a messenger arrived at the Second Continental Congress to announce that three British generals—Sir Henry Clinton, Sir William Howe, and John Burgoyne—had sailed into Boston Harbor aboard HMS *Cerberus* to take command of the British troops already quartered in the colonies. Like Ben, most of the congressional delegates now agreed they had passed the point of no return. Still, many colonists hoped for their ties with Britain to remain strong.

Ben kept notes and quotes in his commonplace book that he thought might help persuade people that they should stand up against the British. He was unsure what to do with all the information he had collected until he met an English immigrant named Thomas Paine. Thomas was about ten years older than Ben and worked as an editor for the *Pennsylvania Magazine*, a monthly publication. He had arrived in Philadelphia from England the year before, bringing with him a letter of introduction from Benjamin Franklin.

Ben and Thomas Paine struck up an instant friendship, and before long the two realized they both saw the same need: a simple pamphlet that would outline the reasons why the colonies should separate from Great Britain. The two also agreed at first that the authors of such a publication should remain anonymous. If word got out as to who authored it, they could be persecuted, and Ben feared for the future of his medical practice. Then he realized that since Thomas had no ties to America, if the public learned he was promoting anti-English ideas, he could simply move away. Ben began encouraging Thomas to author the pamphlet openly. The two men met regularly to talk about how the booklet should be written and what to include in it. Ben gladly passed the notes in his commonplace book along to Thomas.

One week in August 1775, Ben decided to ride his horse north to Princeton, New Jersey, to visit his old college. When he arrived he was invited to stay with Richard Stockton, the man who had visited him in Edinburgh on his way to recruit John Witherspoon to be the next president of the College of New Jersey. Richard was now a judge and had served as a legislator in New Jersey. He lived in a beautiful home called Morven, which was situated on the edge of the college campus. In fact, Ben recalled that the grounds for the College of New Jersey had been donated by Richard's grandfather.

While Ben looked forward to seeing Richard again, it turned out that the person he most enjoyed spending time with was Richard's sixteen-year-old daughter, Julia. Ben vaguely recalled encountering Julia when she was about three years old and he was attending a college commencement service. Julia had wandered into the crowd, and Ben had carried her home to her parents. Now, thirteen years later, the two laughed over the event. Julia had grown into an attractive young woman with long brown hair and dark eyes. But most of all, Ben liked how seriously she listened to sermons. Julia told Ben that John Witherspoon was the best preacher she had ever met. Ben agreed. He liked being with a young woman who had good manners and strong opinions.

When Ben returned to Philadelphia, he wrote to Richard asking for permission to court Julia. Permission was granted, and from then on Ben visited Morven almost every weekend. He and Julia soon fell deeply in love and began planning a wedding.

Between riding back and forth to Princeton, Ben continued to help and encourage Thomas Paine as he wrote his pamphlet. When it was finished, Thomas announced that he thought it should be called *Plain Truth*. Ben considered the proposed title for a while and then countered that *Common Sense* sounded better. Thomas agreed.

At first it was difficult to find a printer who would risk printing the pamphlet, but eventually Ben found a Scottish printer who was not afraid to take the chance. On January 9, 1776, *Common Sense* was published. Ben had hoped that the booklet would make people think. What he didn't realize was that it would be read, copied, and circulated by hand until one in five American colonists from Georgia to New Hampshire either owned or had read a copy.

Two days after the publication of *Common Sense*, on Thursday, January 11, 1776, Benjamin Rush married Julia Stockton at Morven, her family home in Princeton. Following the service, the newlyweds headed back to Philadelphia. After they arrived there, Ben bought a slave named William Grubber to serve him and Julia.*

* This action mystified those who shared the views he had laid out two years before in *An Address to the Inhabitants of the British Settlement in America upon Slave-Keeping*. Why he purchased a slave is lost to history as Benjamin Rush, in all his writings, never set forth his reason for doing so.

Chapter 9

Brothers-in-Arms

Ben made it his business to learn everything he could about what was happening in all thirteen American colonies. Living in Philadelphia gave him an eyewitness view of the Second Continental Congress deliberating in the Pennsylvania State House. Ben spent many hours in homes and taverns listening to and discussing happenings in the congress and the colonies. The more he listened, the surer he became that an all-encompassing war with the British was beginning. In fact, Ben received a letter from William Duer, a member of the Provincial Congress of New York, telling him that the British had hired seventeen thousand mercenaries from Prince Frederick of Hesse-Kassel, Germany. King George III paid thirty marks a head for them, with a promise of thirty marks more for every American soldier they killed, wounded, or captured. Ben wasn't surprised. Prince Frederick was a relative of King George, and the rebellion taking place in Great Britain's American colonies was making the monarchs of other European empires nervous.

Although the rebellion in North America continued to grow, not all colonists wanted to be independent of Great Britain. In fact, some residents were eager to fight on the British side to bring down the American uprising. In early February 1776 a Scotsman named Allan Maclean raised a Loyalist Scottish regiment of sixteen hundred soldiers in North Carolina to fight the Patriots.

In the early morning of February 27, the new regiment was on its way to Wilmington when it came face-to-face with North Carolina's Patriot militia on the opposite side of Moores Creek Bridge. Soldiers from the Loyalist Scottish regiment surged across the bridge, only to discover that the Patriots had removed many of the decking planks and greased the railings. The Loyalist soldiers were trapped on the bridge as the Patriots opened fire, killing thirty men and taking several hundred from the regiment captive. One Patriot soldier was killed and another wounded. It was a small incident, but enough to convince North Carolina to instruct their delegates in the Continental Congress to vote for independence from Great Britain.

In mid-March 1776 the Patriots received more good news. In Massachusetts, General George Washington and his Continental army, made up of various militias, defeated the British at Dorchester

Heights just outside the city of Boston. The British then loaded up their ships anchored in the harbor and sailed away, abandoning Boston. In response to this, the question on everyone's mind was when and where the British would strike again. Spies reported to the members of the Continental Congress that the British ships had sailed to Nova Scotia, where they were preparing to invade New York. With this information in hand, members of the congress made plans for the middle colonies of Virginia and North Carolina to send troops to help the New Englanders fight off the British invasion.

Ben listened and watched over these developments with a physician's concern. He knew many doctors who were serving in the Continental army. His mentor and friend Dr. John Morgan had been made general director and chief physician of the army six months before. Dr. Morgan was now quartered with the army outside Boston. In June 1776 Ben's old friend and traveling companion Dr. Johnathan Potts became the physician in charge of the army on the Canadian border. Even though the two doctors were serving in different areas, the story they told was the same. The Second Continental Congress did not give the armies enough money for supplies of wine, medicines, bandages, food, and bedding. As Ben read their letters, he grew frustrated and wondered what was the point of having an army if you didn't take care of it.

Ben's frustration turned to alarm when he received reports from New York, where the middle colonies had sent troops. The new troops had brought sicknesses with them, including typhoid, smallpox, and dysentery. One-third of the soldiers were now ill—and they hadn't yet faced a single battle. With little money and few staff members, there wasn't much John Morgan could do about the situation. He sent letters to the congress, telling delegates that the surgeons didn't even have enough amputation knives to go around—four surgeons had to share a single knife. In addition, there was no opium to dull the pain of amputation. Ben was appalled. He tried to buy amputation knives with his own money, only to discover that not one blacksmith in Philadelphia could forge them. The blacksmiths had all been ordered instead to make swords for the soldiers.

Part of the problem was that the Americans had to defend over two thousand miles of coastline from British attack. Their colonies were strung along the coast of North America, and the British military had many more ships at its disposal than did the colonists. Like most American colonists, Ben was heartened by the results of a battle that occurred on Sullivan's Island at the entrance to Charleston Harbor in South Carolina. On June 28, 1776, a group of Continental soldiers under the command of William Moultrie were hard at work building a fort when a fleet of British navy ships sailed up on them.

The British ships began a ten-hour bombardment of the nearly completed fort and the island itself. They also landed troops on neighboring Long Island, where the British waited for the tide to recede so they could wade across the channel separating the two islands and overrun the Continental soldiers.

However, the British troops discovered that even at low tide the water in the channel was too deep for them to wade across, so they could not invade and capture Sullivan's Island. Nor could their naval bombardment destroy the new fort, which was built of palmetto logs and sandbags. The ship's cannonballs either sank into the sandbags or bounced off the soft, springy palmetto logs. All the while the American troops fired their cannons at the attacking ships. By the time the British called off their attack, the Americans had inflicted heavy damage on British ships. Ben was encouraged that a ragtag group of Continental soldiers could win the day over well-trained British forces.

On July 1, 1776, Ben's father-in-law, Richard Stockton, and John Witherspoon, whom Ben had helped to recruit to be the president of the College of New Jersey, arrived in Philadelphia. Both men had been elected to represent New Jersey at the Second Continental Congress and had come to take their place among the other delegates. The session of the congress opened that day with a stirring speech by John Adams in favor of independence from Great Britain. That night Richard visited Ben and Julia to tell them that the colonies were going to vote on a motion for independence and were drafting a document that outlined why they were seeking independence. The news delighted Ben.

The next day the delegates voted for independence from Great Britain. The thirteen colonies would merge to form a new country to be known as the United States of America. On Thursday, July 4, the delegates voted to officially adopt the Declaration of Independence, the document prepared by Thomas Jefferson of Virginia, John Adams of Massachusetts, Benjamin Franklin of Pennsylvania, Roger Sherman of Connecticut, and Robert Livingston of New York.

The vote to adopt the Declaration of Independence led to a shake-up in the Pennsylvania delegates to the Second Continental Congress. Some of the older Quakers had been holding out for a peaceful deal with the British. Now they knew that this was not going to happen. The colonies wanted independence and were prepared to fight to the death for it. Pennsylvania's Quaker delegates, who did not believe in fighting in wars, left the Second Continental Congress, and new members were appointed to take their place. One of the new delegates appointed was Benjamin Rush.

Ben attended his first meeting of the Second Continental Congress on July 22, 1776. Of course, he knew what to expect, having had so many conversations with other delegates to the congress. The first thing Ben wanted to debate was the way in which each new state would vote on issues affecting everyone in America. The prevailing view was that each state, regardless of its size, should be entitled to one vote in the congress. On his second day as a delegate at the Second Continental Congress, Ben argued the exact opposite. He believed that every eligible delegate from a state should have a vote and that these votes should be tallied and decisions made. Ben thought this was the fairest way to do things, as it gave each delegate an equal say. Although he spoke eloquently on the matter, his was not a popular view, and the congress decided that the states would cast votes as a single unit.

A week and a half after Ben joined the Second Continental Congress, a copy of the Declaration of Independence, handwritten onto parchment paper, was ready to be signed by the delegates. The members of the congress gathered in a sober mood for the signing. Ben knew that by adding his name to the document he would be committing treason in the eyes of the British. He watched as John Hancock, the president of the congress, called the delegates from each colony up to the desk, where they signed their names in silence.

At one point in the ceremony Colonel Benjamin Harrison turned to Elbridge Gerry of Massachusetts, smiled, and said, "I shall have a great advantage over you, Mr. Gerry, when we are all hung for what we are doing now. From the size and weight of my body I shall die in a few minutes, but from the lightness of your body you will dance in the air an hour or two before you are dead." It was supposed to be a joke, but no one, including Ben, laughed.

Ben watched as Richard Stockton and John Witherspoon went up with the other New Jersey delegates and signed the document. When the Pennsylvania delegates were called to step forward, Robert Morris signed first. Then Ben took the quill from him, dipped it in ink, and signed the Declaration of Independence. Like many others who'd stepped forward to sign, Ben wiped a tear from his cheek.

He then handed the quill to Benjamin Franklin, who signed directly below Ben's signature.

When all fifty-six delegates had signed the document, Ben knew they were now all brothers-in-arms. With their signatures, they had officially put themselves and the colonies they represented in direct opposition to King George III and his Parliament. The delegates knew that the Declaration of Independence would escalate the fighting in North America. And now there could be only one of two outcomes in this fight: America would win its independence from Great Britain, or it would lose and suffer British retaliation, which was sure to be harsh and brutal.

In the Second Continental Congress, Ben was appointed to several committees, including one to improve the quality of gunpowder, another investigating the conditions for prisoners of war, and one preparing a report on the state of the army and navy. Meanwhile, the congress sent Richard Stockton on a grueling horseback ride to Fort Ticonderoga, Saratoga, and Albany, New York, to gather information on what was happening there in the struggle against the British.

No one was surprised when Ben was appointed to the medical committee that was trying to devise efficient ways to get medicines to military hospitals. Ben had many ideas on how they might do this. During August 1776, in his efforts to supply the northern army with provisions and medicine, Ben kept in close contact with John Morgan, who had now been appointed chief doctor as well as supervisor of supplies for the entire Continental army. It soon became clear to Ben that his old mentor had a difficult if not impossible task. There were too few supplies, and the army's surgeons and doctors continually argued over who should do what on the battlefield.

A letter from Dr. Johnathan Potts in Fort George, New York, confirmed Dr. Morgan's complaints:

> The distressing situation of the sick here is not to be described, without clothing, without bedding, or shelter sufficient to keep them from the weather. . . . We have at present upwards of a thousand sick, crowded into sheds and laboring under the various and cruel disorders of dysentries, bilious putrid fevers, and the effects of confluent smallpox. To treat these seriously sick I have only four surgeons and four surgeon's mates, and my medicines are nearly exhausted.

By the end of August news arrived in Philadelphia that the British had landed on Long Island in New York and beaten George Washington and his Continental army back across the East River onto Manhattan Island. A report from Dr. James Tilton on the state of the defeated American troops sent a chill down Ben's spine as he read it:

> The camp is indescribably filthy. All manner of excrementitious matter is scattered indiscriminately throughout the camp so that there is a disagreeable smell everywhere. Sometimes there are no ovens, and flour is served

> instead of bread. Some soldiers try to bake bread on hot stones, and others in ashes, as a result, they become affected with jaundice. Of the army with Washington on the east side of the river there are 15,105 fit for duty. Of the total sick, there were 7,610.

In the meantime, the war news got worse. In mid-September of 1776, much of New York City was burned to the ground. Nathan Hale, a young Patriot spy for the Continental army in New York, was captured and executed by order of General William Howe.

In October, Dr. William Shippen Jr. was put in charge of the medical needs of the Continental army west of the Hudson River, while Dr. John Morgan was given medical charge of the army east of the Hudson River. Ben was shocked by the decision. It was common knowledge that the two doctors had not been able to work together at the Philadelphia hospital. How were they ever going to coordinate their efforts to keep an entire army alive and well?

October 1776 brought troubling news of another sort. Things were not going well in the war with the British. George Washington and his army had been forced to retreat north from New York City to White Plains. There the army took up its position on the high ground. But in the battle that followed, the British forced the Patriots off their high ground, and once more Washington and his army had to retreat farther north.

More bad news from the battlefront arrived in November. Following the defeat of Washington at

White Plains, British forces turned their attention to capturing Fort Washington, the last remaining American stronghold at the northern end of Manhattan Island. Nearly three thousand Continental army soldiers were holed up at the fort under the command of General Nathanael Greene. On November 16, 1776, the British launched a three-pronged attack on the fort. In the face of the withering attack, the American forces surrendered to the British. Fifty-nine Continental soldiers were killed in the fighting, and 2,837 were taken as prisoners of war.

The situation became dire in early December. British forces had chased Washington and his army across New Jersey. Thankfully on December 7 Washington and his men managed to flee across the Delaware River into Pennsylvania, and the British decided not to pursue them. At the same time, spies informed members of the Second Continental Congress that a British force under the command of General William Howe was planning to attack Philadelphia. The congress hurriedly adjourned and made plans to move themselves and their official papers to Baltimore, Maryland.

Soon afterward, Ben accompanied Julia to his cousin Elisha Hall's home in Maryland, where she would be farther away from the approaching British army. Julia had just learned she was expecting a baby in the coming year. Ben was concerned about the stress that the war was having on her and the child she carried.

Once Julia was safely settled at his cousin's house, Ben returned home. Philadelphia felt like a ghost town: shops were shuttered and streets deserted. Those who had somewhere else to go had already evacuated the city in advance of the British arrival. Ben ordered his slave, William Grubber, to load up his books and furniture and arrange for them to be taken by wagon to a friend's house in the country. Ben hoped they would be safe there. On December 20, 1776, Ben packed as many medical supplies as he could into his saddlebags and rode northeast to Bristol to assist General John Cadwalader and the eighteen-hundred-man regiment of the Pennsylvania militia he commanded. The militia had been ordered to reinforce Washington's army.

Washington and his army were encamped about ten miles beyond Bristol. On the afternoon of December 24, Ben, accompanied by Joseph Reed, a young Philadelphia lawyer who was now serving as the army's assistant general, rode out to meet with Washington. The two men spent the night in a farmhouse and rode into the army camp on Christmas morning. Washington greeted Ben warmly and gave him an hour of his time.

Inside Washington's headquarters, Ben could tell that the general was depressed and frustrated with the war effort so far. As a member of the Continental Congress, Ben assured Washington that he had the congress's full support, despite the difficulties he had encountered so far. The general thanked Ben for his and the congress's support as he picked up a copy of the first pamphlet in Thomas Paine's new series of publications called *The American Crisis*. He opened the pamphlet and read the opening paragraph to Ben: "These are the times that try men's souls. The summer soldier and the sunshine patriot will, in this crisis, shrink from the service of his country; but he that stands it *now*, deserves the love and thanks of man and woman. Tyranny, like hell, is not easily conquered; yet we have this consolation with us, that the harder the conflict, the more glorious the triumph."

Ben nodded in agreement with the sage words of his friend. George Washington looked Ben in the eye and agreed that tyranny was not easily conquered, but the colonists must prevail. He then told him that despite the bitter cold, it was time for his army to strike. The conscription period of his soldiers was up on New Year's Day, and he thought that most of the men would give up and go home if they didn't have something to lift their morale and make them want to stay. Washington then quickly outlined how he planned to lead an attack against the German mercenaries—or Hessians, as they were known—whom King George III had hired. The Hessians were stationed across the Delaware River in Trenton, New Jersey, for the winter. The Continental troops and their equipment would cross the river later that night and attack the Hessians in the morning. Since it was the dead of winter, an attack was the last thing they would be expecting.

As he spoke, Washington scribbled on pieces of paper with a quill and then let them flutter to the floor. One of them landed near Ben's feet. Ben looked down and read what the general had written: "Victory or Death."

When the hour was up, Ben wished George Washington good luck crossing the Delaware River under the cover of darkness in preparation for the surprise attack. He then shook Washington's hand, mounted his horse, and rode off.

As he rode back to the militia in Bristol, Ben thought about the strange course of events that had led him to this point in his life. He had considered being a lawyer but had ended up becoming a doctor, and now he was also a politician and member of the Continental Congress. Ben had never thought of working with the army. But for now, that was what he was doing. He wondered if he too might be called to die for the new country they were trying to forge.

Chapter 10

Into Battle

On Christmas Day Ben rejoined General Cadwalader and the Pennsylvania militia regiment at Bristol. That night, despite the intense cold, all eighteen hundred militiamen set out toward Dunk's Ferry. As they marched, Ben learned that General Cadwalader had been ordered to cross the Delaware River with his men and attack the Hessians stationed in Burlington County, New Jersey. This would divert their attention and stop them from reinforcing the other Hessian troops twenty miles away at Trenton when Washington and his army attacked them.

As the men made their way to Dunk's Ferry, Ben wore a winter coat, but the other soldiers were wearing summer uniforms. No one in the Continental Congress had thought to outfit them in winter uniforms. Now it was too late. The men stamped their feet and slapped their arms to keep their circulation going as they prepared to cross the icy Delaware. One battalion after another rowed amid the ice floating on the surface of the river to the other side, where they climbed onto an ice shelf and made their way to solid ground. However, the men were unable to get their cannons across the shelf to the other side of the river. The ice shelf was not thick enough to hold the weight of their cannons.

General Cadwalader gave the order for everyone to cross back over the Delaware and into Pennsylvania. There was no point in going to fight without their cannons. The militiamen would have to try to cross the river again another day. They arrived back at their camp at Bristol at 4:00 a.m.

Back at camp, Ben assumed that Washington and his men had met with the same fate while trying to cross the Delaware. He learned that he'd assumed wrong when later that morning a messenger arrived and told them that Washington and twenty-four hundred soldiers had all crossed the Delaware and were poised to march on Trenton.

Like everyone else in the militia camp at Bristol, Ben waited eagerly for more news. It came early that evening. Washington's troops had marched the ten miles to Trenton and attacked at eight in the morning. The Hessian soldiers had been stunned. Most were still in bed after drinking and partying on Christmas Day. They ran out into the streets, many of them in their nightclothes and stockinged feet. Johann Rall, the Hessian commander, was killed by a musket ball, and the Hessians surrendered after a short but vicious battle.

Washington had intended to march on to Princeton, but since Cadwalader's Pennsylvania militiamen and Colonel Thomas Ewing's troops from Maryland hadn't been able to cross the Delaware, he ordered his men to retreat. By four in the afternoon they were safely back at McKonkey's Ferry, where they had crossed the Delaware River the night before. They brought with them nine hundred Hessian prisoners of war and their entire store of provisions: dried and salted meat, tons of flour, ale, and much-needed shoes, boots, clothing, and bedding. Ben was delighted by the news. He knew how much a victory meant to the bedraggled Continental army.

On December 29, Ben accompanied General Cadwalader and the militia across the Delaware River. This time they and their cannons made it across safely, and they marched through Bordenton and on to the village of Crosswicks. In his journal Ben wrote, "There is no soil so dear to a soldier as that which is marked with the footsteps of a fleeing enemy—everything looks well. Our army increases daily, and our troops are impatient to avenge the injuries done to the state of New Jersey."

One of the injuries done to the state of New Jersey, Ben learned the next day, had to do with his father-in-law, Richard Stockton. On November 30, 1776, Richard had evacuated his family to the home of John Covenhoven in Hopewell, New Jersey, eight miles northwest of Princeton. He felt they would be safe there, away from the oncoming British forces marching across New Jersey. Three days later, however, Richard was discovered in Hopewell and seized by a group of local Loyalists, who marched him to Perth Amboy and handed him over to the British. Learning that he was one of the signers of the Declaration of Independence, the British imprisoned him and treated him harshly before transferring him to Provost Jail in New York City. Richard Stockton was put in irons like a common criminal, and on some days he was given no food. Ben learned that the harsh treatment was causing his father-in-law's health to deteriorate rapidly.

Upon hearing this troubling news, Ben wrote to the Continental Congress declaring, "I have heard from good authority that my much-honored father-in-law, who is now a prisoner with General Howe, suffers many indignities and hardships from the enemy, from which not only his rank, but his being a man, ought to exempt him." He went on to request that the members of the congress do whatever they could to secure Richard Stockton's release, suggesting that perhaps a prisoner exchange might be in order.

By now Washington's army and Colonel Thomas Ewing's troops had also crossed the river. These Patriot divisions were now set up on the east side of the Delaware, with Washington and his men camped at Trenton.

While the Pennsylvania militia waited at Crosswicks for further orders, on New Year's Day 1777 Ben rode to Trenton to congratulate General Washington. Soon after Ben arrived, Washington confided in him that spies had warned him that an army of eight thousand British men under the command of General Charles Cornwallis had made it as far as Princeton, ten miles away, and were planning to attack Trenton. In response, Washington had ordered his men to build a three-mile-long wall of earth parallel to the south bank of the Assunpink Creek.

While in Trenton, Ben dined with his old friend General Hugh Mercer, a Scottish immigrant and doctor from Virginia. During the evening, Washington received word that British troops were preparing for an immediate attack on Trenton. General Mercer excused himself from his dinner with Ben and went off to a council of war with the other generals. An hour later Ben was called into the council so they could ask him what he thought should be done. Ben didn't have enough experience with war to tell Washington what to do, but he did say that the Pennsylvania militia would be honored to fight alongside his troops. That seemed to settle the case. Washington immediately wrote to General Cadwalader and asked Ben to deliver the letter to him in Crosswicks as fast as possible.

By ten o'clock Ben was back on his horse and headed southeast to Crosswicks, accompanied by a sergeant from the Philadelphia Light Horse troops. The two arrived in the militia camp in Crosswicks at one in the morning after a three-hour ride. General Cadwalader was already asleep, and Ben asked the general's aide to wake him. As soon as the general read the letter, he ordered everyone to rise and prepare to march for Trenton immediately.

Ben rode back to Trenton ahead of the militia and fell asleep in a borrowed bed around seven in the morning. Not long after falling asleep, he was awakened by the sound of gunshots. Ben leaped out of bed and rushed outside. "What's going on?" he asked General Arthur St. Clair.

"The enemy is advancing," the general replied.

Ben felt his heart racing. "What are you going to do?"

"Fight them," General St. Clair said matter-of-factly, buckling his sword to his belt.

Ben nodded. Although he was on several committees in the Continental Congress related to the war, he had never witnessed any of the fighting firsthand. Within hours he was sure that that was about to change.

It was early afternoon before the battle got under way in earnest. Cornwallis and eight thousand men attacked Trenton. Three times they attempted to cross the bridge over Assunpink Creek, and each time Washington and his six-thousand-man army beat the British back.

As the battle raged on, Ben and several other doctors set up a field hospital in a commandeered farmhouse outside Trenton. Wounded Patriot fighters were taken there for treatment. It was an eye-opening time for Ben. In the distance he could hear cannon fire and the sound of men fighting. Before him were the mangled, damaged bodies of the wounded. The right hand of the first man Ben treated hung on a flap of skin at the end of his arm. The man had been hit by a cannonball. Ben cut the skin and removed the mangled hand from the end of the man's arm. He then cleaned and bandaged the wound and laid the soldier on a pile of straw in the house to rest and recover. After darkness fell, Ben kept treating the severely wounded by lamplight. When the fighting stopped for the night, the flow of wounded men being brought to the field hospital abated. Late in the evening Ben and the other doctors lay down on the straw to sleep.

Around four in the morning, Dr. John Cochran was dispatched from the field hospital to Trenton to learn what Washington and his generals were planning so that the doctors could be ready for it. Dr. Cochran returned to the field hospital an hour later to report that he had been unable to find Washington's army. The British appeared to be back in control of Trenton, and the Continental army was nowhere to be found. Ben assumed the Patriots had withdrawn to Bordentown. He knew the doctors and patients in the field hospital had to catch up with the army as soon as possible. They were in a precarious position—a makeshift field hospital filled with injured men, and no one to protect them.

Wagons were rounded up, hay spread in the back of them, and the injured men loaded on top of the hay. Ben mounted his horse and led the strange procession of wagons bearing wounded men toward Bordentown. It was slow going, but when they arrived, they learned that Washington and his men had, in fact, secretly abandoned Trenton in the middle of the night and pushed on to Princeton, where they defeated the British army. Ben turned the wagons around and headed toward Princeton, twelve miles to the north.

As Ben and his procession of wagons approached Princeton, they traveled past fields still red with pools of blood from the fighting. The town of Princeton itself lay in ruins. Even Nassau Hall at the College of New Jersey where Ben had lived and attended college was badly damaged. The town church had been burned and the homes had been plundered, including Morven, the home of his wife's family. It wasn't just property the British were reckless with. They also had been brutal with people, even bayoneting a Patriot army chaplain. Ben wondered how his father-in-law was faring at the hands of the British.

The next day Ben learned from George Washington that General Mercer had been severely wounded in the fighting at Princeton and had been captured by the British. Knowing of the friendship between the general and Ben, Washington asked if Ben would be willing to approach the British army camp under a flag of truce and ask General Cornwallis if he could attend to Hugh Mercer. Ben agreed and, accompanied by Captain George Lewis, General Washington's aide, set off on horseback for the British camp.

British General Cornwallis granted Ben permission to treat General Mercer. Ben found his friend laid out in the nearby house of Thomas Clarke, a local Quaker whose home had been requisitioned by the British. General Mercer was badly injured by British soldiers before being captured. When he was arrested, the British had wrongly thought they had captured George Washington. Ben set to work cleaning and dressing the general's wounds. He also sent a message to Washington informing him that he had located General Mercer, that the general was responding to treatment, and that Ben didn't think Mercer would die from his severe wounds.

Lying next to Hugh Mercer in Thomas Clarke's requisitioned home was a wounded British officer named Captain McPherson. When the captain learned who Ben was, he looked up and asked, "Are you the same Benjamin Rush who was a friend of the Scotsman William Leslie?"

"Yes," Ben replied. "I knew him and his family well in Edinburgh. Do you have word of him?"

Captain McPherson nodded. "He was killed here at Thomas Clarke's farm. We loaded his body onto one of our baggage wagons, but the Patriots captured it. I don't know what happened to him after that. Your people must have him now."

Ben excused himself and walked outside. Tears streamed down his cheeks as he thought about the wonderful times he had enjoyed with the Leslie family in Scotland. For the first time he regretted that the Patriots had won a battle over the British, since it had cost the life of a close friend.

Later that day Ben had a visit from a military messenger, who informed him that Continental soldiers had indeed found William Leslie's body in the baggage wagon. They also found a letter in William's uniform pocket saying that William was a good friend of Benjamin Rush's and that if he was injured in battle or taken prisoner to please let Ben know. Again Ben brushed tears from his cheeks. It was hard to believe that William was dead. He came from such a good, noble family and was fighting for what he believed in. It just happened to be the exact opposite of what Ben thought was right.

After a brief silence, the messenger spoke. "I can assure you that General Washington and General Mifflin made sure that William Leslie was buried in the churchyard at Pluckamin with full military honors."

Ben promised himself that when the war was over, he would visit Pluckamin and place a headstone on William's grave. He would also write to William's family and describe his final moments. But there wasn't time for that now. He had to attend to General Hugh Mercer. Ben stayed at the British camp for a week until he felt sure that the general was out of danger. Amid the sorrow surrounding the death of William Leslie, Ben almost forgot that it was his thirty-first birthday.

During his stay among the British, Ben witnessed firsthand the way they tended their wounded. Despite his present dislike for the British, he was impressed with their level of care. When General Cornwallis began his army's retreat from Princeton, he made sure that a surgeon and five privates were left behind to continue caring for those who could not be moved. And every British captain visited his wounded troops once a week to make sure they were being tended to properly. Ben reminded himself that the British had fought many wars and had much better protocols and routines than the ragtag Continental army.

On January 11, 1777, Ben accompanied General Mercer back into Princeton. Once there, he made his way to Morven. He walked slowly up the carriageway toward the house, thinking of the many times he'd walked the same path with Julia when they were courting. As he walked, Ben noticed an old man sitting on the front porch. He waved to him, and the old man stood, stooped and frail. Ben suddenly realized that the old man was Richard Stockton! His father-in-law was safe. He ran to the steps, and the two men embraced.

The reunion was a sad one. Richard looked twenty years older than he had before. He told Ben how he'd been put in irons in prison at Perth Amboy and treated like a common criminal. Then in prison in New York, he'd been starved and left in an unheated cell with only bars for windows. Richard coughed as he told the story of his ordeal. This alarmed Ben. Richard told Ben that Morven had been occupied by the British General Cornwallis, whose troops had stolen everything from the house. The property hauled away was worth at least five thousand pounds.

The two men took a slow walk around the house and grounds. Ben could clearly see that his father-in-law was right. Everything that could be moved was gone—tables, beds, sheets, drapes, jars of preserved food, cows, pigs, chickens, and grain. All the books from Richard's great library had been burned. Morven was now just an empty shell. The only consolation, as far as his father-in-law was concerned, was that his wife and family had not had to see what had become of their home. As far as Richard knew they were still safe in Hopewell.

Ben tried to talk Richard into going with him to Maryland to visit Julia, but his father-in-law would have none of it. "Thank God they did not burn the place down," Richard told Ben. "I will stay and try to put it back together. This is my home." Ben wasn't so sure the man's broken health would allow it. Still, his father-in-law was a stubborn man. Ben embraced Richard and rode off to be with Julia. After visiting her, he proceeded on to Baltimore to rejoin the Continental Congress.

Chapter 11

Surgeon General

After a brief visit with Julia, Ben rode on to Baltimore, arriving there during the last week of January 1777. He had never seen Baltimore before, and his first impressions were grim. It had been raining for a week before he arrived, and the city streets were clogged with mud. Worse still, the war was causing stunning inflation. Everything from a single night's lodging to a glass of ale now cost double what it had in Philadelphia.

Bad news also awaited Ben in Baltimore. General Hugh Mercer, whom he'd been sure was making a swift recovery from his wounds, had died four days after Ben left him. A small wound under his arm had become infected, causing Mercer to die in agony. The news put Ben in a dark mood that didn't lift throughout his first days back in the Continental Congress.

To Ben, the congressional delegates all seemed at odds with each other over the many decisions needing to be made. The biggest disagreement among the members of the congress was over inflation. Ben supported a motion to raise the interest rate to 6 percent, but the arguments for and against doing this seemed to go on endlessly. Given all these concerns and all the infighting, Ben realized that it was going to be a difficult task to get the members of the congress to care about the well-being of wounded and sick soldiers. This was especially so when he learned that his old friend Dr. John Morgan had been dismissed as the medical director of the Continental army and replaced by Dr. William Shippen Jr.

The decision to make Dr. Shippen medical director alarmed Ben on many levels. Ben personally preferred Dr. Morgan to Dr. Shippen, but he was also concerned that the current system gave one man all the power to buy and distribute all the supplies for the army's medical needs. Ben felt it would be much more prudent to have one man in charge of ordering and payment and a doctor in charge of distribution to the various branches of the army. He believed this would prevent someone like Dr. Shippen from abusing the system.

Ben did not think, however, that such a system would be implemented anytime soon. William Shippen Jr. had powerful connections. His wife, Alice, was the daughter of Thomas and Hannah Lee of Virginia. As such, she belonged to one of the wealthiest and most influential families in the American colonies. In fact, four of Alice's brothers were directly involved in the war. Richard and Francis Lee were the only brothers to sign the Declaration of Independence, and William and Arthur Lee served as agents of the Continental Congress in Europe. To stand against William Shippen Jr. was to stand against the Lees of Virginia. To Ben, that was a daunting thought.

One of the few pleasures Ben enjoyed in Baltimore was spending time with his brother Jacob, who had also fled Philadelphia and was working as a lawyer alongside the Continental Congress.

John Adams had arrived in Baltimore from a visit home to Massachusetts just a few days before Ben. The two men enjoyed long conversations. One of the topics they often discussed was the Pennsylvania constitution, which had been approved on September 28, 1776. Both men agreed that the model laid out for governing Pennsylvania in the new constitution was flawed.

The new Pennsylvania constitution gave a nod to William Penn's governing dictum that "all men have a right to life, liberty, property, happiness, and safety." It granted the right to vote to the sons of freeholders and all free men over the age of twenty-one who had lived in the state for one year and had paid public taxes. But it also created a unicameral, or single-chamber, legislature. This legislature was granted all powers necessary to operate a free state, which included appointing judges for a term of seven years. The constitution imagined that the citizens of

Pennsylvania would act as a check on the legislature by forming a council of censors. The council would be convened every seven years to recommend the repeal of any unjust laws passed by the legislature and suggest amendments to the state constitution.

Although Ben applauded the way the new Pennsylvania constitution extended the right to vote, he believed that the system of governance it set up was unworkable. As far as he could see, there were no real checks and balances on the legislature. In fact, the document gave the legislature power to overturn the decisions of judges and juries it did not like. The legislature could, if it chose, also confiscate the property of people it suspected of being Loyalist sympathizers. The council of censors had no real power to check the legislature on a day-to-day or year-to-year basis.

The situation with the new Pennsylvania constitution posed a difficult problem for Ben. Since he didn't agree with it, he spoke out against it. In so doing, he knew he could easily be voted out of the Continental Congress and replaced by a delegate from Pennsylvania who did favor the new constitution.

John Adams and Ben found even more common ground in their thoughts on General George Washington. Given Washington's victories over the British at Trenton and Princeton, many members of the Continental Congress were in favor of giving him almost total power over the Continental army. John and Ben both felt that this was a bad idea. Ben agreed that Washington was to be honored for the vital role he was performing in fighting the British, but Washington had derived his power to wage that war from the Continental Congress. Thus, Ben believed that decisions such as appointing generals to the Continental army should continue to be made by the congress. Washington was free to appoint officers to lower ranks in the field and draw up plans to conduct battles against the British according to the situation and his expertise. However, he must remain under the authority of the Continental Congress and be answerable to the congress for his actions.

Ben's hunch about the consequences of speaking out about the Pennsylvania constitution proved correct. At the end of February 1777, the Pennsylvania Assembly did not reelect him as one of their delegates to the Continental Congress. The current session of the congress adjourned on February 27. Since there was no imminent threat of invasion of Philadelphia by the British, the next session of the congress would reconvene in Philadelphia on March 4, 1777, when the new Pennsylvania delegates would be seated. For Ben, it was time to visit Julia and await the birth of their baby.

Meanwhile, soldiers in the Continental army were still dying at an alarming rate, not just from fighting, but also because of disease and poor general health in the various army camps. Already there had been five thousand cases of smallpox in the northern army, and other communicable diseases spread and thrived among the soldiers. Ben attributed much of this to the woefully inept state of management in the army's medical department. In response, he set to work writing a long article about what could be done to keep soldiers healthy. Ben offered many suggestions, including a near vegetarian diet, bathing twice a week, camping far away from swamps and marshlands, and washing spoons and bowls after every use. "Directions on Preserving the Health of Soldiers" was first published in the *Pennsylvania Packet*, where it took up the entire front page of the newspaper's April 22, 1777, edition.

Just before "Directions on Preserving the Health of Soldiers" was published, the Continental Congress called on Ben to become the surgeon general of the Middle Department of the Continental army, which extended from the Hudson River to the Potomac River. Ben accepted the position but said he would be staying close to home until his and Julia's baby was born.

The following month, a deadly hospital fever broke out among wounded troops being housed at the Alms House in Philadelphia. Ben hurried there to see what he could do to help. By the time he arrived, many of the soldiers and several of their doctors had died. Ben felt that overcrowding at the Alms House was one of the main factors leading to the spread of the disease. He sent an urgent request to Dr. William Shippen Jr. to provide more housing for the sick men. The request was denied, which made Ben furious. He wondered if William Shippen Jr. cared about the health of the soldiers at all.

Ben was still in Philadelphia trying to sort out the problems at the Alms House when word reached him that Julia was nearing the time to give birth. Ben headed to Rush Hill, eleven miles outside Philadelphia, where his mother and sister Rebecca lived and where he had moved Julia. He arrived at Rush Hill just in time for the birth of a son in the early hours of July 17, 1777. Ben and Julia named their new son John, after Ben's grandfather. A week after the baby's birth, Ben turned his attention more fully to his duties as surgeon general of the Middle Department of the Continental army. Using Princeton as his base, he began inspecting the various military hospitals in New Jersey.

By mid-August, as Ben continued his inspections, it became clear that the British were preparing to attack Philadelphia. On August 24, 1777, the Continental army was on the move, and Ben moved with it. Over ten thousand American soldiers marched through Philadelphia, were ferried across the Schuylkill River, and then headed on to meet the approaching British forces at Brandywine Creek, twenty-four miles southwest of Philadelphia.

The Continental army forces arrayed themselves for battle at Chadds Ford, where they expected the British to cross Brandywine Creek. The British forces, under the command of General William Howe, arrived at the creek, and the battle began on September 11, 1777.

As the battle raged, Ben set up a field hospital in the rear and began treating the wounded soldiers who were brought in. At one point, as Ben went to help carry some of the wounded soldiers from the battlefield, he was nearly captured by the British.

From the doorway of the hospital tent he could see the fighting, and as the day wore on, things were not going well for the Continental forces. General Howe had marched the bulk of his troops farther up Brandywine Creek, where they had crossed over at another ford and then began attacking the right flank of Washington's army from the rear. This had forced three divisions to shift position to try to block the British flanking maneuver. At the same time, more British forces launched a direct attack at Chadds Ford on the American forces' left flank.

It was obvious to Ben that after eleven hours of fighting, the British had beaten the Continental army in the battle. Ben wasn't surprised when Washington ordered his troops to retreat to the northeast. Ben and the other medical staff quickly packed up their field hospital and, along with the wounded soldiers, fled with the retreating army.

The defeat at Brandywine Creek took its toll on the Continental army. Three hundred soldiers were killed, six hundred were wounded, and four hundred were captured by the British. Two days after the battle, Washington sent Ben and several army surgeons under a flag of truce to General Howe's camp. They were to attend to the wounded American soldiers who had been left on the battlefield and taken captive by the British.

As he had been after the Battle of Princeton, Ben was impressed at the way the British cared for the sick and wounded. Even the captured Americans were well fed and given lots of fresh vegetables. The British surgeons and doctors were competent and tended each soldier with respect. British doctors were also vigilant to make sure that communicable diseases did not spread in their camp. They forbade the British soldiers to touch the blankets of wounded Americans lest they catch or spread a disease a soldier might have. Every ten wounded men had their own orderly, and officers insisted the wounded be well cared for.

In the British camp there seemed to be a strict sense of order and discipline. As Ben observed how well the British ran their field hospital, he couldn't help but become angry that William Shippen Jr. and the members of the Continental Congress could not duplicate such a medical system for their own soldiers.

On September 26, 1777, General William Howe led his British troops into Philadelphia to take control of the city. The Continental Congress had already fled west to the village of York, Pennsylvania. The next battle against the British that Ben participated in was the Battle of Germantown on October 4, 1777. This was another loss for the Americans, with 152 soldiers killed in the fighting and 521 wounded.

Following the battle, there was nowhere to house the wounded men. Ben requisitioned farmhouses, churches, and courthouses to serve as makeshift hospitals. The largest of these was the Moravian Brethren House at Bethlehem, Pennsylvania. When Ben later went to inspect the hospital in Bethlehem, he was shocked by what he found. Over seven hundred men were crammed into the Brethren House, a space meant for only a third of that number. Not only that, the place was filthy, and sanitation for the men was virtually nonexistent. Ben knew that disease would flourish in such an unclean and over-full place. Already signs of typhus were appearing among the men.

Ben came away from the visit shaken and appalled by what he'd seen. He focused blame for the situation on one man—William Shippen Jr. Dr. Shippen was the person charged with procuring adequate supplies for the army's medical department and making sure they were distributed to the various hospitals. As far as Ben was concerned, the conditions and lack of supplies at Bethlehem demonstrated just how out of touch and incompetent William Shippen was. Despite being a doctor, the man didn't seem to care about the welfare of soldiers.

After his visit to the Bethlehem field hospital, Ben wrote to John Adams and other members of the Continental Congress, complaining about the abysmal conditions wounded soldiers were enduring. In doing so, Ben alerted them to how inadequately William Shippen Jr. was doing his job. The Continental army needed and deserved a medical system like that of the British army. Ben also complained about the drunkenness of some of the majors and brigadiers in the Continental army and their unwillingness to lead in battle. He recommended that any military leader who got drunk more than once a day or lagged more than five hundred yards behind his troops on the battlefield should be severely punished.

Ben hoped that sounding the alarm would bring change to the army's medical department. However, he was concerned about William Shippen's family connections in the congress, which made it unlikely that the congress would act to discipline Dr. Shippen. But Ben knew he had to try to make a difference for the good of wounded soldiers. He just wished he came from a more wealthy and connected family who could use their influence with the congress. John Adams sympathized with Ben over the situation, but he wrote to say that he was burdened with so many other responsibilities in the congress that he couldn't do much to bring about the change Ben sought.

On December 13, 1777, Ben wrote to Congressman William Duer of New York, asking him to send representatives to see with their own eyes what was going on in the field hospitals. As he sent the letter, Ben began to wonder if he might need to resign from his position with the army. If he could not convince members of the Continental Congress to bring about change in the Continental army's medical department, he saw little point in staying in his position.

Ben received no satisfactory responses to his letters. On December 26 he wrote directly to George Washington, who was now camped with his army for the winter at Valley Forge, Pennsylvania, twenty miles northwest of Philadelphia. In the letter he tried to draw Washington's attention to the poor state of the medical department. He asked him to use his position as commander in chief of the Continental army to bring order and discipline to the army's medical department.

When he received no reply from Washington by January 12, 1778, Ben wrote an unsigned letter to

Patrick Henry, who was now the governor of Virginia, outlining his complaints. That same day, after sending off the letter to Patrick Henry, Ben received a reply from George Washington. In his letter the general acknowledged Ben's concerns and told him he would do all in his power to remedy the situation. He would discreetly send a field officer to visit the hospitals Ben spoke of and attempt to establish proper order in them. Washington also informed Ben that he had communicated the substance of his letter to Dr. William Shippen Jr.

Ben wasn't surprised when he was summoned to appear before the Continental Congress on January 26, 1778, to elaborate on his charges against Dr. Shippen. He also realized that only one of them could stay in the army. Either he would be dismissed or the doctor would be brought up on charges.

Ben brought with him to the hearing letters from other army doctors. They confirmed that Dr. Shippen had in one instance purchased six casks of wine for 150 pounds. Instead of allowing the wine to be used for wounded soldiers, he had sold it for five hundred pounds and pocketed the money. In fact, four military surgeons put their necks on the line when they signed a statement that they believed William Shippen Jr. siphoned off about a third of the wine, sugar, and molasses he ordered for the hospitals and sold large quantities of poultry and venison for his personal profit.

Even though Ben's friend and Continental Congress member John Witherspoon presided over the hearing, William Shippen Jr. and his Lee relatives convinced the congressional committee that things were, in fact, running smoothly under Dr. Shippen's command. According to them, nothing needed to be changed regarding procurement and the way the army's medical department was run. Ben was disappointed, particularly for the wounded soldiers who would not receive the kind of medical care they deserved. He knew he could not continue to work in such a broken system, and on January, 30, 1778, he resigned as surgeon general of the Middle Department of the Continental army.

Ben felt depressed, especially after hearing reports coming from Valley Forge. Conditions among the men were so bad that Ben wondered if there would be anyone left to fight by the spring. To make matters worse, his beloved city of Philadelphia was still in the hands of the British. He returned to Julia and his son John, hoping that by some miracle the tide of war would turn in the Americans' favor.

Chapter 12

Victory

On June 8, 1778, the Patriots received news they'd been desperately hoping for. After spending nine months comfortably quartered in Philadelphia while Washington's men suffered at Valley Forge, the fifteen thousand British troops stationed in the city began evacuating. Four months before, on February 6, 1778, France formally recognized the United States of America as a sovereign nation and signed a military alliance pledging to assist the Americans in the fight with the British. The British responded by declaring war on France on March 17, 1778. Now word had arrived that the French navy was on its way across the Atlantic Ocean to battle the British. As a result, the British war strategy had changed to meet this new threat, and they marched their troops out of Philadelphia.

Ben was ecstatic that the British were leaving. *Surely,* he thought, *the war has turned in the Patriots' favor.* He took his newly pregnant wife and John back to his cousin Elisha Hall's home in Maryland to be out of the British troops' path of retreat. Ben then hurried back to Philadelphia. He had a lot of work to do. The British had left the city in disarray. Trash was piled up on the sidewalks, the hospital had been stripped of supplies, and the homes that the soldiers had used as their barracks were a total mess.

Once back in Philadelphia, Ben began keeping a special journal in which he recorded his observations on seasonal diseases and weather conditions that seemed to bring them or stop them. He soon decided that some epidemics were worse at the times when large amounts of land were cleared. And since the British forces who had occupied Philadelphia had cut down so many surrounding trees for firewood, the number of sick people in the city had tripled. Ben was sure that this had something to do with the flooding that occurred when new meadows were created. He also noted that during windy times in August and September there were more cases of fever. He recommended that people keep their windows closed during this time. One thing was clear to Ben: whatever the reason, stagnant water was bad for people's health.

Gradually things returned to normal in Philadelphia. Julia and John came back to the city to live with Ben, and the Continental Congress returned as well. George Washington had appointed Major General Benedict Arnold to be the military governor of Philadelphia. General Arnold was a top Patriot leader who had been severely injured in two important battles.

Ben resumed his medical practice along with presenting chemistry lectures at the reopened College of Philadelphia. But that summer he became seriously ill with typhoid. As Ben hovered near death, he decided to write a will. However, with Drs. John Redman and John Morgan at his side, Ben passed through the worst of his sickness and began a slow recovery. Nevertheless, the stress of it all turned his hair gray, something he had not expected to occur at age thirty-two.

In November, Ben faced another challenge. His father-in-law, whom Ben greatly respected, came to him for medical advice. Forty-eight-year-old Richard Stockton had a sore on his lip that would not heal. Ben took one look and knew that it was cancer. He sent his father-in-law to the best surgeon in town, and the sore was removed. But Ben's fears were realized when a new cancerous growth appeared in Richard's throat. This time he could do nothing about it. His father-in-law was in terrible pain. Ben knew that it was only a matter of time before Richard would succumb to the cancer and die.

On January 1, 1779, Ben's daughter, Anne, was born. By this time people in Philadelphia appeared to be thoroughly tired of the war. It had dragged on for nearly four years. Since there was no fighting in the city, many wealthy families took up their old habits of lavish balls and garden parties. Also at this time, in a dazzling wedding ceremony, Major

General Benedict Arnold married Peggy Shippen, the eighteen-year-old great-niece of William Shippen Jr.

Peggy's father, Edward Shippen, was a Loyalist sympathizer who had done business with the British while they occupied Philadelphia. Although Ben was concerned that a Patriot general was marrying the daughter of a known Loyalist sympathizer, he was more concerned about the schemes that Benedict Arnold and many other military and political leaders had devised to make money for themselves from the war. These men had secretly set up their own companies to be middlemen between those who had war provisions, from beans and molasses to oxen and gunpowder, and the war office, which desperately needed the supplies. As the middlemen, they inflated the prices, pocketing large sums of money. At other times, political and military leaders used their knowledge of military movements to buy up all the supplies in a particular part of a state so that when the army arrived, they would have to buy the goods at the new, higher prices.

Such war profiteering sickened Ben, especially when he thought of the Continental army soldiers who were dying for lack of good food and warm clothes. He fervently wished the war would end before he lost all respect for those fighting on the Americans' side. Inflation was out of control. It now cost ten times as much to buy things as it had before the war. The Continental Congress had issued "Continental" currency to keep the states afloat, but it was paper money that was constantly being devalued. Hardly any of Ben's patients were able to pay their bills, and when they did, they paid in Continental currency. Ben collected 1,060 Continental pounds that year, but it was worth only fifty pounds in silver or gold coins.

In May 1779 mobs took to the streets in Philadelphia, looting the houses and businesses of the rich people they suspected were making huge profits from the war and causing the massive inflation they labored under. Five months later, a mob marched to the house of a lawyer who had defended a Loyalist in court. Mayhem broke out and seven people were killed and nineteen injured. It was a sobering day for the residents of Philadelphia. It left Ben, like many others, wondering whether the Patriots could govern themselves effectively or if they were too divided for that.

Ben was concerned about what would happen if the Patriots won the war. In particular, he didn't like the amount of attention General Washington received or the control he wielded. Ben thought it was dangerous for one man to have that much power. He wrote, "Where is the republican spirit in our country? Monarchies are illuminated by a sun, but republics should be illuminated only by constellations of great men."

During October 1779 Ben attended a service at First Baptist Church. The preacher was the Reverend Elhanan Winchester, who had recently been called as the new pastor of the church. He was drawing large crowds who wanted to hear him speak. Often the church building filled to overflowing, as it did the night Ben attended. The meeting had to reconvene in the largest house in Philadelphia. Ben immediately liked Elhanan Winchester, who became a regular visitor at the Rush home. Eventually, though, Winchester was asked to leave the Baptist denomination, and he started the first Unitarian church in Philadelphia. Ben became an enthusiastic member of the new congregation.

In March 1780 Ben received some news about Dr. William Shippen Jr. General Washington was in the process of court-martialing him on charges that he sold hospital stores and kept the money, did not visit hospitals, and wrote false reports. Ben testified at his trial, but William Shippen had powerful friends. He was acquitted of the charges by one vote, although the army noted that it did believe the charges were justified. William Shippen Jr. went back to work, but he soon discovered that the public had lost confidence in his leadership. He decided to resign rather than be forced out of the army. It was not the ending Ben had hoped for, but he was glad that William Shippen was no longer in charge of army hospitals and soldiers' welfare.

It was a depressing time as the war continued into its fifth year. Ben found it increasingly difficult to make enough money to support his wife and two children. In February he learned that another baby was on the way. By May the British still occupied New York City and also had captured Charleston, South Carolina. In mid-August, the Philadelphia newspapers reported that the Continental army had lost the Battle of Camden in South Carolina. At the end of that month, Julia gave birth to their third child, a son whom they named Richard.

September 1780 saw Ben rocked to his core like so many others when news arrived that Benedict Arnold, now serving as commander of the fort at West Point on the Hudson River in New York, had been spying for the British and was planning to hand over control of West Point to them for twenty thousand pounds. If his message had not been intercepted and the plot discovered, this would have given the British the victory they needed to win the war. Things suddenly looked precarious for the Continental army.

Five months later, on February 28, 1781, Ben's father-in-law, Richard Stockton, died. He had never fully recovered his health or his wealth after his capture and imprisonment by the British in New Jersey and then New York, yet it was the advancing cancer that actually claimed his life. It was hard for Ben not to feel bitter as he stood beside his father-in-law's coffin and thought how much Richard had given for his new country and how much had been forcibly taken from him.

Meanwhile, the economic woes of the newly independent states grew worse. The Continental currency was declared worthless and was no longer used. Instead, Congress appointed Robert Morris to be the superintendent of finance in the United States, ordering him to open a bank. Morris then issued his own currency, backing the new notes with his personal money.

At last, Ben heard the news he'd been longing for. British commander General Charles Cornwallis had led 7,200 soldiers out of New York and into Virginia. The American forces, led by the Marquis de Lafayette of France, kept them occupied until Washington could arrive with reinforcements. The British army was beaten back to Yorktown, Virginia, where it was trapped and besieged by Washington's and Lafayette's troops and thirty French navy ships that had arrived in Chesapeake Bay.

Ben had predicted that the war would end in Chesapeake Bay, and he was right. On October 24, 1781, word reached Philadelphia that General Cornwallis had surrendered his troops to Washington and Lafayette at Yorktown. The fighting of the Revolutionary War was over! Guns boomed from every ship in and around Philadelphia in celebration, and Ben and Julia took their children to church to give thanks to God. That night parties filled the city streets.

When all the celebrations had ended, Ben had time to think back over the past six long years. When the war started, he was an optimistic twenty-nine-year-old medical doctor with a new wife and a bright future. Now he was thirty-five years old with three children and another one on the way. He knew a lot more about the inner workings of government and the tough decisions that needed to be made in times of war. He had seen corruption and greed close up, and he'd also seen men willingly give their lives for their new country. Ben was glad it was all behind him now. He looked forward to spending more time with his family and building his medical practice.

On January 7, 1782, three days after Ben's thirty-sixth birthday and nearly three months after the British surrender at Yorktown, Julia gave birth to another baby girl, whom she and Ben named Susannah. Sadly, Susannah was dead by spring. Though he was grieved, Ben tried to be grateful that he and Julia still had three living children. He knew that many of his patients had suffered through the deaths of many more of their children.

For the residents of North America, the previous seven years had been defined by war against the British, in which over one hundred thousand American men bore arms and around thirty thousand perished on the battlefield or in field hospitals. Others who survived were left with terrible disabilities: loss of sight, loss of arms or legs, and for some the loss of their minds, something Ben knew he wanted to study more.

During the war, Philadelphia had functioned as the capital of the United States. In June 1783, the Continental Congress moved to Princeton, New Jersey, where the country's government was set up in the library on the second floor of Nassau Hall. Ben visited Princeton often. He remembered studying in the very spot where the laws of the new republic were being hammered out.

As he thought about it, Ben knew that winning the war was only the beginning. He wrote,

> There is nothing more common than to confound the terms of *the American revolution* with those of *the late American war*. The

> American war is over, but this is far from being the case with the American revolution. On the contrary, nothing but the first act of the great drama is closed. It remains yet to establish and perfect our new forms of government; and to prepare the principles, morals, and manners of our citizens, for these forms of government, after they are established and brought to perfection.

For Ben, the real work of forming a new country free of tyranny and oppression had only just begun. Although he had convinced himself he could stay away from politics and public policy, the lure of shaping the United States of America proved too strong. Before long Ben was back in the thick of politics: writing letters, meeting with congressmen and other civic leaders, and trying to bring about the kind of social change he felt the new country needed to survive.

Chapter 13

Helping Shape the New Nation

In 1783 Ben was appointed to the staff of Pennsylvania Hospital, where he supervised patient care and held lectures. At the same time, Julia gave birth to another daughter, Elizabeth, who, like Susannah before her, survived only a few months.

During this time Ben also turned his attention to education, specifically college education. He was already a member of the faculty of the University of the State of Pennsylvania, as the College of Philadelphia was now known. He was concerned, however, that a new country like the United States needed to educate more of its population. Ben was particularly concerned about educating farmers' sons in rural areas.

Casting around for a good location for a new college, Ben's attention was drawn to the village of

Carlisle, 120 miles west of Philadelphia on the American frontier. The Carlisle Grammar School had been founded there in 1773, and now several of the city's residents wanted to see the grammar school developed into a college. Ben worked hard securing money to buy more land and hire faculty for the new college.

On September 9, 1783, the new institution was formally chartered by the Pennsylvania legislature and given the name Dickinson College, named after John Dickinson, a signer of the Declaration of Independence who was now president of Pennsylvania. Dickinson was also known as the "Penman of the Revolution" for the twelve letters, titled *Letters from a Farmer in Pennsylvania to the Inhabitants of the British Colonies*, that he had written and published in the *Pennsylvania Chronicle and Universal Advertiser* in 1767 and 1768.

Ben selected a Scottish Presbyterian minister, Dr. Charles Nesbit, to be the first president of Dickinson College. The college's motto was *Pietate et doctrina tuta libertas*—"Freedom is made safe through character and learning." The school's seal featured a liberty cap, a telescope, and an open Bible. Ben had thought hard before proposing the motto. He knew that the new form of democratic government they were embarking upon in the United States could survive only if people understood how it worked. He insisted that every student's education include civics: "A course of lectures on government, including not only the principles of constitutions but [also] practical legislation, will be very . . . necessary for our republic."

Six weeks later, news reached Philadelphia that on September 3, 1783, Benjamin Franklin, John Jay, John Adams, and David Hartley had signed the Treaty of Paris in France. The treaty marked the official end of the war with Great Britain and recognized that the United States of America was now a separate and independent country. The treaty had been signed six days before Dickinson College received its charter, making Dickinson the first college chartered in the new United States of America.

During 1784, for the third year in a row, Julia gave birth to a daughter, whom she and Ben named Mary. Unlike the two previous daughters, Mary survived infancy. The Rushes were now a family with four children. Their oldest child, John, was an intelligent, sensitive child of seven. Ben felt sure that he would make a wonderful doctor one day.

One thing Ben was adamant about was that freedom from British rule should mean freedom for all people. During the Revolutionary War, all thirteen American colonies had banned the importation of slaves along with all other imports from Great Britain. After the war, Massachusetts and New Hampshire banned slavery, while Pennsylvania, Rhode Island, and Connecticut agreed to phase it out. In addition, many slaves who had fought in the war were now free.

Ben was a strong supporter of freeing all slaves. He believed that slaves capable of looking after themselves should be freed, while those who were too ill or feeble to work should remain with their owners, to be treated humanely until they died. Not everyone agreed with Ben's position. Politicians in the southern states felt that they could not continue their way of life without slaves to work their plantations, and even in the north many relied on slaves to take care of their homes and children.

In 1774, following the publication of Ben's pamphlet *An Address to the Inhabitants of the British Settlement in America upon Slave-Keeping*, Ben and Quaker philanthropist James Pemberton founded the Society for the Relief of Free Negroes Unlawfully Held in Bondage, the first antislavery society in the American colonies. But the work of the newly formed society had been interrupted by the war with Great Britain. Now in 1784 with the war over, Ben felt it was time to revive the Society for the Relief of Free Negroes Unlawfully Held in Bondage, or the Pennsylvania Abolitionist Society, as most people referred to it. People rallied to the cause, though many of them found it hard to understand how Ben could advocate for the freeing of slaves while he still owned William Grubber, his personal slave. Ben did not enlighten them as to why he thought he should be able to own a slave at the same time he was fighting for their freedom.

In 1785, after nearly a decade spent living in France, where he represented the interests of the United States, Benjamin Franklin returned to Philadelphia. Upon Dr. Franklin's return, Ben began visiting him and catching him up on all the changes and improvements taking place in the city since the United States won independence. While Dr. Franklin had been proslavery earlier in his life, now he was in favor of freeing all slaves. After talking with Franklin, Ben realized that it was long past time for him to free his slave. Shortly after Ben gave William Grubber his freedom, Benjamin Franklin agreed to become president of the Pennsylvania Abolitionist Society while Ben served as the society's secretary. On October 18, 1785, Benjamin Franklin was also unanimously elected to be the sixth president of Pennsylvania, replacing John Dickinson. Ben hoped that Franklin's new position would draw more attention to the abolition of slavery in North America.

In January 1786 Ben turned forty years old. Just over two months later, on March 15, Julia gave birth to another child, a son whom they named James. The Rush household now included five children.

Most of Ben's spare time now went into helping shape the new republic. He wrote and published papers on all manner of topics. One thing that concerned Ben greatly was the way in which the mentally ill were treated. Many doctors and citizens believed mental illness to be caused by demon possession. However, after observing many mentally ill patients, Ben came to a different conclusion. He believed that mental illness was often caused by diseases in the brain and should be thought of in the same way that people thought of diseases of the rest of the body.

Ben believed that bloodletting and large doses of mercury chloride, also called calomel, should be used to treat insanity. He wrote about one of his techniques for getting patients to take calomel. "It is sometimes difficult to prevail upon patients in this state of madness, or even to compel them, to take mercury in any of the ways in which it is usually administered. In these cases, I have succeeded by sprinkling a few grains of calomel daily upon a piece of bread, and afterwards spreading over it, a thin covering of butter."

Ben was also concerned about the appalling conditions in which mentally ill patients were hospitalized. As far as he was concerned, mentally ill patients should not be kept in damp or dark conditions, nor should they be left chained up for long periods of time. It made more sense to him to give these patients useful things to do, such as gardening, woodwork, or sewing whenever possible. Ben began to agitate for separate mental wards to be built at hospitals, including Pennsylvania Hospital, where patients could be kept in more humane conditions.

The health of the poor in Philadelphia also concerned Ben. Since he sat on the board of Pennsylvania Hospital, if a patient treated at the hospital was too poor to pay his or her bill, Ben would forgive it. He knew that this wasn't a popular thing to do and that many of the other doctors treating patients at the hospital did not do it. What the poor needed, Ben decided, was their own medical clinic. During 1786 he set to work starting one, calling it The Philadelphia Dispensary for the Medical Relief of the Poor. When the clinic opened its doors in a single room on Strawberry Alley, it was the first free medical clinic in the United States. Ben gave hundreds of hours of his time to treating poor patients and donated much of the medicine he dispensed from the clinic.

In addition to his commitments to Pennsylvania Hospital, the Pennsylvania Abolitionist Society, the new Philadelphia Dispensary, and his private practice, in 1787 Ben involved himself in the founding of the College of Physicians of Philadelphia. Dr. John Redman, under whom Ben had served his medical apprenticeship, was elected the first president of the new organization, and Ben was among the twelve senior members. The members of the college met once a month to discuss the latest medical ideas and advances. They also began buying and collecting books to create the largest medical library in North America.

Also during 1787, Ben joined with a group of influential men from Philadelphia to found the Philadelphia Society for Alleviating the Miseries of Public Prison. Ben deemed public punishment—such as putting a person on display in stocks, tying him or her to a whipping post, or hanging him or her in public—both gruesome and counterproductive. He felt that these practices only pandered to society's bloodlust. Instead he proposed private confinement, labor, solitude, and religious instruction for criminals. He believed that all prisons should have a place of worship, a garden, and a workshop. He also believed that all prisoners should be taught a trade and paid for the work they produced. This was very different from the forced labor, rough treatment, and solitary confinement that many prisoners faced in jail. Under Ben's urging, plans were drawn up for the first state penitentiary, the Walnut Street Prison, and building began.

Julia Rush schooled the Rush children at home until each child reached the age of twelve or thirteen. Ben took a deep interest in what his children learned. He believed a good education was an essential start in life, not just for his children but for all American citizens. At the time there were no free schools for poor children, but Ben wanted that to change. He made no distinction between boys and girls when it came to education. He believed strongly that every child should have the opportunity to be educated. Ben wrote an essay about his ideas on education. It was published in the March 28, 1787, edition of Philadelphia's *Independent Gazetteer* under the headline "To the Citizens of Philadelphia: A Plan for Free Schools."

In the essay Ben noted that children should be taught to read and write English and, when required by their parents, the German language. The girls were to be instructed in needlework, knitting, and spinning, as well as in academic subjects along with the boys. Both sexes were to be "carefully instructed in the principles and obligations of the Christian religion," as this would "make them dutiful children, teachable scholars, and, afterwards, good apprentices, good husbands, good wives, honest mechanics, industrious farmers, peaceable sailors, and, in everything that relates to this country, good citizens." To do this in the simplest manner, Ben felt that each denomination of church should run its own schools, paid for by property taxes. He ended his essay with the admonition, "Let not the health and lives of the poor exhaust the whole stock of our benevolence. Their morals are of more consequence to society than their health or lives, and their minds must exist forever. 'Blessed is he that considereth the poor: the LORD will deliver him in time of trouble.'"

In addition to working together to abolish slavery, Ben and Dr. Franklin often talked about the need for post offices across the entire United States. Benjamin Rush went as far as to think that the future of the new union depended upon it. He wrote,

> For the purpose of diffusing knowledge, as well as extending the living principle of government to every part of the United States—every state, city, county, village, and township in the union—should be tied together by means of the post-office. This is the true non-electric wire of government. It is the only means of conveying heat and light to every individual in the federal commonwealth. Sweden lost her liberties, says the Abbe Raynal, because her citizens were so scattered, that they had no means of acting in concert with each other. It should be a constant injunction to the postmasters, to convey newspapers free of all charge for postage. They are not only the vehicles of knowledge and intelligence, but the centinels of the liberties of our country.

Benjamin Franklin, at the age of eighty-one, was appointed a delegate to the Constitutional Convention, which began on May 25, 1787. The convention took place at the Pennsylvania State House in

Philadelphia, now known as Independence Hall since the Declaration of Independence had been adopted there eleven years before. George Washington was selected to serve as president of the convention by unanimous vote. The purpose of the convention was to draw up a constitution and new framework of government that would meld the newly independent states into a union while still allowing each state as much independence as possible to make decisions about their residents and economies.

As the Constitutional Convention progressed, Benjamin Franklin would fill Ben in on some of the items being considered and discussed. Ben listened carefully. He had spent a long time pondering the right structure for the new government. He wanted to see the convention come up with a constitution and government that would not falter in ten or twenty years but would last for centuries. This, he believed, would require every citizen to become involved. Ben gave an impassioned speech in which he asked the public to consider how they could help build up their new country.

> I am extremely sorry to find a passion for retirement so universal among the patriots and heroes of the war. They resemble skilful mariners, who, after exerting themselves to preserve a ship from sinking in a storm, in the middle of the ocean, drop asleep as soon as the waves subside, and leave the care of their lives and property, during the remainder of the voyage, to sailors, without knowledge or experience. Every man in a republic

is public property. His time and talents—his youth—his manhood—his old age—nay more, life, all, belong to his country.

PATRIOTS of 1774, 1775, 1778—HEROES of 1778, 1779, 1780! come forward! your country demands your services!—Philosophers and friends to mankind, come forward! your country demands your studies and speculations! Lovers of peace and order, who declined taking part in the late war, come forward! your country forgives your timidity, and demands your influence and advice! Hear her proclaiming, in sighs and groans, in her governments, in her finances, in her trade, in her manufactures, in her morals, and in her manners, "THE REVOLUTION IS NOT OVER!"

The drafted Constitution for the United States of America received the unanimous approval of the state delegations at the Constitutional Convention and was signed on September 15, 1787.

On November 8, 1787, Julia Rush gave birth again, delivering another son, whom they named William. The baby survived two months, dying on January 15, 1788, eleven days after Ben's forty-second birthday.

A month after William's birth, on December 7, 1787, Delaware became the first state to ratify the new Constitution. Before the year was out, Pennsylvania and New Jersey had also ratified the Constitution.

Ben continued to use his writing skills to make people think about all kinds of issues. No topic was too large or too small for him to write about. He weighed in on plans to set up a federal university, on ways to set up a newspaper, on the influence of the American Revolution in Europe, and on the challenges of old age.

In 1788 Ben was honored to be elected as a Fellow of the American Academy of Arts and Sciences. The following year, another son, Benjamin, was born to Julia and Ben, but the baby lived only three weeks. Around the same time, Ben received word that his old colleague, Dr. John Morgan, was seriously ill. He rushed to his old mentor's side, but it was too late. John had already died. As Ben looked around the hovel where John's body lay, he realized that Dr. Morgan had died a poor, lonely man. It was a sad ending for such a distinguished person. Ben concluded that the doctor had never recovered from his long struggle with Dr. William Shippen Jr. during the war.

Following John Morgan's death, Ben inherited the doctor's chair in the theory and practice of medicine at the University of the State of Pennsylvania's medical school. He gave up his chair in chemistry to take up the new post.

On February 4, 1789, George Washington was unanimously elected the first president of the United States by the United States electoral college. Ben's good friend John Adams was elected the first vice president.

The following year, on April 17, 1790, Benjamin Franklin died at the age of eighty-four. Ben attended his funeral along with about twenty thousand other Americans whom Franklin had impacted during his lifetime. Ben knew he would miss talking with his old friend about new ideas to help the poor and needy.

From May 25 to June 8, 1790, a group of American Universalist preachers and laymen from Pennsylvania, New Jersey, Virginia, and Massachusetts held a convention in Philadelphia. The group drafted two documents, a Rule of Faith and a Plan of Church Government, which they planned to use as the basis upon which to establish their own church. They then submitted each document to Ben for his opinion.

Most of Ben's writing was just that—writing. But one of his most popular pieces included a chart that Ben called The Moral Thermometer. The chart was included in a book Ben wrote called *An Inquiry into the Effects of Spirituous Liquors on the Human Body and the Mind.* The book was published in Boston in 1790 by Thomas and Andrews. Ben devised the Moral Thermometer chart to depict the horrors that awaited drunkards. He placed both moderate drinkers and abstainers at the top of his moral thermometer. As the scale on the thermometer descended below "Intemperance," Ben began to chart the "Vices," "Diseases," and "Punishments" associated with each kind of strong drink. "Strong Punch" caused the vice of "Idleness," "Gout" as a disease, and "Debt" as a punishment, whereas at the bottom of the thermometer, "Pepper in Rum" led to "Murder and Suicide" as a vice, "Apoplexy and Death" as a disease, and "The Gallows" as a punishment.

An Inquiry into the Effects of Spirituous Liquors on the Human Body and the Mind sold briskly from the time it was published. Ben believed that "a people corrupted with strong drink cannot long be a free people." He hoped that his book would start a temperance movement so that by the twentieth century "a drunkard . . . will be as infamous in society as a liar or a thief, and the use of spirits as uncommon in families as a drink made of a solution of arsenic or a decoction of hemlock."

In January 1791, Ben turned forty-five years old. The following month, on February 18, Julia gave birth to another son. They named the child Benjamin and hoped he would survive longer than the previous baby to whom they had given the same name. Ben and Julia now had six children. Their oldest son, John, was nearly fourteen and ready to head off to Princeton to study at the College of New Jersey, following in his father's footsteps.

Ben's sister Rebecca, who had recently been widowed again, asked to come and live with her brother and his growing family, now numbering eight. Ben's mother, Susanna, also came to live with the family. It was time for the Rushes to find a bigger house that would easily accommodate them all. In spring, the extended family moved into a house at 83 Walnut Street. The following year, Julia gave birth to a daughter, whom they named Julia after her.

Each year Ben came up with new things to write about in the hope of helping shape the culture and morality of the new nation. In 1791 he had read a paper before the American Philosophical Society that hypothesized that black skin color came from a form of leprosy. Ben was sure that soon a treatment would be devised that would "cure" blacks and make them white. In the meantime, he urged black people and white people not to marry, as it could lead to the spread of the disease.

Ben also thought that different racial groups were more or less likely to get specific diseases. He studied Indians and pronounced that while they were susceptible to fevers of all types, they didn't appear to get scurvy or rotten teeth, as did many of Ben's white patients. And he was sure that black people hardly ever contracted yellow fever. What Ben didn't know was that the following year, in the summer of 1793, his theory was going to be tested in ways he could never have imagined.

Chapter 14

The Stricken City

On August 21, 1793, Ben sat down late at night to write to his wife. Julia had taken the children to Morven, her family's estate in Princeton, New Jersey, to stay with her mother for the summer. Ben began,

> My dear Julia—To prevent your being deceived by reports respecting the sickliness of our city, I sit down at a late hour, and much fatigued, to inform you that a malignant fever has broken out in Water Street between Arch and Race Streets which has already carried off twelve persons within the space which has been mentioned. It is supposed to have been produced by some damaged coffee which had putrefied on one of the wharves near the

middle of the above district. The disease is violent and of short duration. In one case it killed in twelve hours, and in no case has it lasted more than four days. Among its victims is Mrs. LeMaigre. I have attended three of the persons who have died with it, and seven or eight who have survived, or who are I hope recovering from it.

As yet it has not spread thro' any parts of the city which are beyond the reach of the putrid exhalation which first produced it. If it should, I shall give you notice, that you may remain where you are till you receive further advice and information from me.

Four days later Ben updated Julia on the situation in another letter.

My dear Julia—Since my letter to you of Friday, the fever has assumed a most alarming appearance. It not only mocks in most instances the power of medicine, but has spread through several parts of the city remote from the spot where it originated. Water Street between Arch and Race streets is nearly desolated by it. . . . In one house I lost two patients last night, a respectable young merchant and his only child. His wife is frantic this evening with grief. Five other persons died in the neighborhood yesterday afternoon and four more last night in Kensington. . . .

Many people are flying from the city, and some by my advice. . . . [Pray for me.] I enjoy

> good health and uncommon tranquility of mind. While I depend upon divine protection, and feel that at present I live, move, and have my being in a more especial manner in God alone, I do not neglect to use every precaution that experience has discovered, to prevent taking the infection. I even strive to subdue my sympathy for my patients, otherwise I should sink under the accumulated loads of misery I am obliged to contemplate. You can recollect how much the loss of a single patient once a month used to affect me. Judge then how I must feel, in hearing every morning of the death of three or four.

Ben put down his pen and rubbed his eyes. He was tired, very tired. It seemed that nothing he did could help keep the terrible plague of yellow fever from enveloping Philadelphia. Now, in mid-August, local churches were digging twenty graves a day to bury the dead. To make matters worse, no one could agree on where the disease had come from. The College of Physicians of Philadelphia called an emergency meeting to discuss the matter. The members of the college fell into two camps. The first group believed that yellow fever had been brought to the city by the fleet of ships carrying two thousand French refugees from the French West Indian colony of Saint-Domingue. The American Revolution had inspired a revolution in France, which in turn fueled a revolution and slave revolt in Saint-Domingue. Hundreds of slave owners and Europeans had been killed, and those who survived had fled to the east coast of North America, some even bringing their black slaves with them. By the time the ships arrived in the port of Philadelphia, many of the passengers were sick and dying. Soon afterward, the fever began spreading along the waterfront.

A second group of members of the College of Physicians theorized that the fever came from the sloop *Amelia*, one of the ships from Saint-Domingue. It had arrived carrying a cargo of coffee beans that had spoiled. The coffee from the *Amelia* was dumped on Ball's Wharf in Philadelphia, where it slowly rotted. Ben and many other members of the college were sure that the fever was the result of miasma, that is, all kinds of foul air. This included the smell of rotting coffee along with the stagnant ponds of water that formed in the summer months when the creeks around the city dried up.

By the end of August 1793, 325 citizens of Philadelphia had died of the disease, and that number was rising every day. Ben's mother and sister, along with his five apprentices and two house servants, worked day and night to help Ben tend to as many patients as possible. Most of those who were left in the city were poor. Almost anyone with the money to leave had already fled Philadelphia, except for a few men and women whose conscience caused them to stay and help those who were suffering.

Ben was grateful that Mayor Matthew Clarkson was one of these people. The mayor worked alongside the physicians to do whatever he could to end the plague and bring relief to the citizens of Philadelphia. Despite the mayor's efforts, yellow fever continued to rage throughout the city. When he visited sick wives whose husbands had already died, Ben realized that more needed to be done. The men's corpses still lay in their beds, as there was no one to carry them from the house and bury them. Small children were trapped inside their homes, surrounded by sick adults who were too ill to care for them.

Ben recalled that he had not yet seen any black people with yellow fever. This fit with his theory that most black people were immune to the disease. An idea formed in Ben's mind: why not ask members of the Free African Society, which assisted the twenty-five hundred free black people living in Philadelphia, if they could help? Men and women of the society could be trained to give simple treatments and carry away dead bodies for burial without risking their own lives. Ben approached three friends in the organization, Richard Allen, William Gray, and Absalom Jones, imploring them to step in and help the sick.

The leaders of the Free African Society agreed to do whatever they could to help the stricken city, even if it meant helping those who had previously been slaveholders. They quickly divided the city into quadrants and walked down every street and alleyway, knocking on doors to find out if any sick people or dead bodies were inside the homes. They worked tirelessly to build simple coffins, load up the dead, and transport them to mass graves, where they were laid to rest. Ben trained several women to let blood and give medicines to the seriously ill.

Despite the best efforts of everyone in Philadelphia, the epidemic grew worse, and ideas on how to cure it grew more desperate. People seldom left their homes, and when they did, they wore bags of camphor around their necks or swung tarred rope in front of them. They chewed raw garlic, and even the youngest children smoked cigars in the hope that it would disinfect their lungs. The streets of the city were soon filled with the smell of gunpowder as citizens shot rifles into the streets, believing that the gunpowder would purify the air. This practice soon became dangerous, and Mayor Clarkson ordered a stop to it. Instead he authorized a militia group to pull a cannon around the city streets firing it every few feet. This way, the mayor argued, the citizens would know where the shots were coming from and have time to duck out of the way to safety.

Ben's methods for treatment were also getting more extreme. He soaked blankets in hot vinegar and wrapped patients' legs in them. He took another doctor's advice and doused patients with buckets of ice cold water as they sat naked in a tub. And, of course, he continued his bleeding and purging of patients. But nothing helped. The spread of the yellow fever appeared to be unstoppable.

From the second-story windows of his house, Ben could see ships anchored in the Delaware River, not wanting to enter Philadelphia. Even if the captain of a ship did wish to tie his vessel up at one of the city's docks, the docks were already crowded with ships that had no workers to unload them. Because of this, supplies in the stores began to run down. Most stores in the city had closed because their owners had fled Philadelphia or died. Schools and banks were closed, and there was no one to handle the mail, which was simply left in a hallway at the University of the State of Pennsylvania. Those who were well enough and thought it worth the risk of being out in public picked through the mail to find letters addressed to them.

For Ben, his beloved city of Philadelphia had become a human wasteland. The poor were dumped at a building known as Ricketts Circus, where they were left to die without any help. Wives locked their sick husbands out of the house, and children roamed the streets begging for someone to come and carry their dead parents from their houses. Some mothers locked themselves and their children inside to keep safe but then ran out of food.

During September 1793, the yellow fever epidemic grew even worse. Mayor Clarkson ordered churches to stop tolling their bells as they marked the death of over one hundred people a day. Public funerals and other church services were stopped so the disease would not spread from person to person. The state legislature cut short its September session, and its members fled the city after a dead body was found on the steps of the State House.

Even those with no money and nowhere to go tried to flee the city. The roads were crowded, but these refugees were often turned back by armed militias who did not want "fugitives" from Philadelphia infecting their towns. Ben spent every spare moment trying to come up with a more effective treatment for the disease. Eventually he turned to an old file of documents Benjamin Franklin had given him before his death. As he flicked through the file, he noticed a report written by John Mitchell, a British doctor who had observed a severe outbreak of yellow fever in Virginia in 1741. Ben read the report, eager to discover what kind of cure Dr. Mitchell suggested for treating the disease. According to the doctor, a patient's body must be rid of deadly humors as quickly as possible, using the most powerful means available: extreme amounts of blood must be drawn off and the strongest purgatives used.

Ben jotted down notes as he read and then set to work. Dr. Mitchell warned that his treatment for yellow fever could not be administered by fainthearted doctors. It was kill or cure: patients must be brought near death for them to have a chance at survival.

The first half of the treatment was bloodletting. Although Ben still routinely bled patients, he now realized he had to take twice as much blood as he had previously taken. For the second part of the treatment, Dr. Mitchell suggested extreme purging. Ben knew just how to achieve this. He combined the strongest dose of mercury—ten grains—with ten grains of jalap, a drug made from a Mexican root that emptied the bowels quickly and forcefully.

By mid-September, Ben needed to try his own cure. He became ill and asked two of his apprentices to bleed and purge him. Afterward he lay in bed for three days, drifting in and out of consciousness, before showing signs of recovery. Not long afterward he was well enough to sit up on his own. At the same time, Ben's apprentices were stricken with yellow fever. Then Ben's mother and his sister,

Rebecca, became ill. The only person in the house well enough to look after any of them was a twelve-year-old servant boy named Peter.

Thankfully, the Free African Society sent two black women to care for them all. But within a week, three of Ben's promising apprentices had died, as had Rebecca. This was a bitter blow for Ben. Of Rebecca's death, he wrote, "She was a truly excellent woman. I never saw her angry, nor heard her speak ill of any one. She died full of faith and hope of happiness beyond the grave." Soon after burying his sister, Ben suffered a relapse of the disease and was not able to leave the house again until early October. By then, the stifling summer heat had given way to the first cool breezes of fall, and people had begun returning to Philadelphia's empty streets and abandoned homes. The worst of the yellow fever epidemic was over.

Ben learned that over four thousand people had died of yellow fever in Philadelphia during the summer months, and over twenty thousand people had fled the city. He was grateful that his wife and children had avoided the sickness and was glad when they could return home from Princeton. His eldest son John, however, stayed behind, as he was still studying at the College of New Jersey.

Ben learned something else from the yellow fever epidemic in Philadelphia. He learned that black people were not immune to the disease. It was a month before yellow fever began showing up among the volunteers from the Free African Society who were doing everything they could to help the disease-ravaged city and its residents. Yet even though some members of the Free African Society died of yellow fever, Ben was amazed at how many of the society's members continued to help, despite the risk of catching the disease. He would never forget how unselfish they had been nor the good they had done.

Late in the fall, Ben's eldest son John Rush arrived home from college in disgrace. He had been caught playing cards and gambling for money. This was bad enough, but to make things worse, John had been doing it on a Sunday. Ben and Julia were beside themselves with concern. How could their son do such a terrible thing? John was an intelligent young man, who as far has Ben was concerned had thrown away a wonderful learning opportunity. Ben refused to let John return to Princeton to resume his studies. He tried to reason with his son, but John was surly and uninterested in anything Ben had to say. While deeply disappointed by his son's actions, Ben took John on as an assistant and taught him about medical matters.

The following year, 1794, Ben was elected a foreign member of the Royal Swedish Academy of Sciences, which he felt was a great honor.

On August 1, 1795, Julia gave birth to yet another son, whom they named Samuel. This brought the number of Rush children living in the household to eight, though John left home soon after Samuel's birth. He found a job as a ship's surgeon aboard a sloop headed to Calcutta, India. Both Ben and Julia were relieved when their oldest son left. John had become a bad influence on the younger children, and they hoped that with the discipline aboard ship, John might somehow turn his life around.

Two years later, in 1797, Ben got a part-time job. Following the Revolution, the United States had to create a single currency to replace the individual currencies used by each of the former colonies. In 1792, the United States Congress had passed the Mint Act, which created the United States dollar as the country's standard unit of money. The act also established the United States Mint in Philadelphia and regulated the coinage of the country. Now, five years after the passing of the act, Ben was nominated to be treasurer of the mint. It was a part-time position that called for a man with an honest reputation and excellent record-keeping skills. Ben fit the profile perfectly and was awarded the job.

Also in 1797, on March 4, after serving two four-year terms as the new nation's first president, George Washington retired from the office. Throughout his presidency he had worked hard to oversee the establishment of a strong, well-financed national government. Ben admired all that Washington had accomplished through his time as president. He hoped his old friend John Adams, who was elected to be the second president of the United States, would build upon what Washington had done. Ben and John Adams had continued to maintain a strong relationship through letter writing.

On March 12, 1799, Ben and Julia's oldest daughter, Anne, was married to the Honorable Ross Cuthbert at Christ Church in Philadelphia. Ross had studied in France and completed his law degree in Philadelphia. He was the heir to a large estate in Quebec, Canada. Everyone except Ben's oldest son, John, attended the wedding. By now John had enlisted in the United States Navy as a surgeon and was currently serving aboard the USS *Ganges* in the Quasi War, a series of skirmishes between the French and American navies following the United States' refusal to pay back loans to France. The United States argued that with the toppling of the French monarchy during the French Revolution, the country had no obligation to continue repaying its debt to France, since it had been owed to a previous French regime.

For several years leading up to this point, Ben had faced a severe personal trial. An English writer and politician named William Cobbett, who had been hounded out of England, took aim at Ben. He hated the idea that America was a free democratic country, and he did whatever he could to harass Samuel Adams, Thomas Paine, Thomas Jefferson, and most of all, Ben. For Ben, the harassment grew more intense after the yellow fever epidemic in Philadelphia, when William began accusing Ben of bleeding his patients to the point of death. Although Ben had been desperately trying to save their lives, William pointed out that other doctors had taken a much less drastic approach.

Over the years, Ben began wondering if William's personal hatred of him would ever abate. The man simply would not give up, going so far as to label Ben a "poisonous trans-Atlantic quack." Ben's medical practice began to dwindle as William's attacks grew more vocal.

Ben decided that he would have to sue William for libel if he ever hoped to be rid of the man and his slander. In early December 1799, the court found William Cobbett guilty and ordered him to pay Ben eight thousand dollars for libeling and harassing him. Ben was relieved. It had been an exhausting fight for him, and he was glad it was over.

Then just as the dawn of a new century drew close, the United States was plunged into mourning over the death of George Washington on December 14, 1799. He was sixty-seven years of age. News of Washington's death sent Ben into a time of reverie. He thought back to the time during the Revolutionary War when he had ridden out to visit George Washington right before the daring Battle of Trenton. Ben thought of the terrible conditions under which he had seen the Continental soldiers laboring. And he thought about the great and final triumph Washington had had over the British at Yorktown. Over the years Ben had had disagreements with Washington, but there was no doubt in his mind that the people of the United States owed Washington a great debt for all he had done to bring the new republic to fruition.

Ben also had a flood of other memories that he wanted to describe to his family, especially now that Anne was expecting her first child, Ben's first grandchild, in the new year. Ben picked up a quill and began writing *Travels through life: or an account of sundry incidents and events in the life of Benjamin Rush . . . written for the use of his children.* He began, "My dear children—My life has been a variegated one. Under a conviction that I shall not live to give its details to the younger branches of the family, I have concluded to put upon paper a few incidents that may perhaps afford entertainment and instruction to them when I am no more."

Chapter 15

A Better Place for Everyone

Ben was still busy writing his autobiography for his children when news arrived of the birth of his first grandchild. James Cuthbert had been born on January 7, 1800. Later that year, Ben's second oldest son, Richard, passed the Pennsylvania Bar exam and became a lawyer in Philadelphia at the age of twenty.

The year 1800 was also another presidential election year in the United States. As in the election of 1796, John Adams, the current president representing the Federalist Party, and Thomas Jefferson, representing the Democratic-Republican Party, were running against each other. Lots of nasty accusations were made during the campaign, with the Democratic-Republicans accusing the Federalists of wanting closer ties to the British monarchy, while the Federalists labeled Thomas Jefferson a godless man who wanted the United States to be aligned too closely with France. After much arguing over the way the election was carried out, Jefferson was declared the winner. On March 4, 1801, Jefferson was sworn in as president in the Capitol building in the nation's new capital city, Washington, DC.

Two months later, on May 11, much to everyone's surprise, Julia Rush gave birth to her thirteenth baby, another son, whom they named William. By now Ben was fifty-five years old, and with some effort he prepared to begin the process of helping raise another child. Later that year, Ben and Julia's daughter Anne gave birth to a baby girl. She and her husband, Ross, named the child Julia. Sadly, baby Julia lived only a few months.

Although he now felt many aches and pains, Ben continued to pursue his many interests, making detailed notes as he did so.

On March 3, 1803, Ben received a letter from President Thomas Jefferson. He opened it and read,

> Dear Sir,
>
> I wish to mention to you in confidence that I have obtained authority from Congress to undertake the long desired object of exploring the Missouri & whatever river, heading with that, leads into the Western ocean. About 10 chosen woodsmen headed by Capt. Lewis my secretary, will set out on it immediately & probably accomplish it in two seasons. Capt. Lewis is brave, prudent, habituated to the woods, &

familiar with Indian manners & character. He is not regularly educated, but he possesses a great mass of accurate observation on all the subjects of nature which present themselves here, & will therefore readily select those only in his new route which shall be new. He has qualified himself for those observations of longitude & latitude necessary to fix the points of the line he will go over. It would be very useful to state for him those objects on which it is most desirable he should bring us information. For this purpose, I ask the favor of you to prepare some notes of such particulars as may occur in his journey & which you think should draw his attention & enquiry. He will be in Philadelphia about 2 or 3 weeks hence & will wait on you.

. . . I pray you to accept assurances of my affectionate friendship & sincere respect.

Thomas Jefferson

Ben was excited by the opportunity Jefferson had extended to him. He began preparing a list of medicines he thought Captain Meriwether Lewis and the men on his expedition might need to keep themselves healthy in a wide range of situations. He calculated that they would need six hundred Rush pills, or thunderclaps, as they were more commonly known. These pills were made up of six parts mercury to one part chlorine and were guaranteed to move even the most blocked digestive system. Ben also anticipated that thirty other kinds of drugs, along with lancets, syringes, bandages, tourniquets, and forceps would be needed. If the men were going to be gone for two years, there was no telling what medical needs they might have.

Ben also hoped that the upcoming expedition would answer some of his questions about the health and lifestyles of native tribes. He made a list of questions to give to Captain Lewis that included the following:

- What are the acute diseases of the Indians? Is the bilious fever ever attended with a black vomit?
- The state of the pulse as to *frequency* in the morning, at noon, and at night, before and after eating?
- Are artificial discharges of blood ever used among them?
- In what manner do they induce sweating? Do they ever use volunteer fasting? At what time do they use their baths?
- Is suicide common among them?
- Is murder common among them, and do they punish it with death?
- Do they use animal sacrifices in their worship?

Next Ben made a list of ways Captain Lewis could keep his men healthy, including the following:

- Flannel worn next to the skin, especially in wet weather.
- Wear shoes without heels.

- Where salt cannot be had with your meat, seep it a day or two in common lye.
- When you feel the least indisposition, fasting and rest; and diluting drinks for a few hours, take a sweat, and if costive [constipated] take a purge of two pills every four hours until they [the bowels] operate freely.

In late May 1803, Captain Meriwether Lewis paid Ben a visit. Ben outfitted him with the complete medical kit he had put together for the expedition. He also furnished him with the notes on how to keep his men healthy and the long list of questions about the Indians. The two men talked for a long time, with Ben urging the captain to keep detailed notes on everything he saw and did, especially regarding the Indians and their customs.

It was another year before the expedition, now officially named the Corps of Discovery and placed under the joint leadership of Meriwether Lewis and William Clark, set out toward the west to see what lay beyond the edge of the current maps of North America. The Corps of Discovery did not return until September 1806. As Ben read their reports, he was amazed to learn that only one member of the expedition had died, and that from natural causes, probably a ruptured appendix, which Ben knew was impossible for any doctor to treat. The medical kit Ben had prepared for the expedition, and the men it was designed to keep alive, had now crossed the entire continent of North America and returned. It was a proud moment for Ben.

In January 1806, Ben turned sixty years old, and time seemed to be rushing by. Old friends died more frequently now. In 1808 Dr. John Redman died. Ben remembered him for his kindness and his dedication to his patients.

During 1808, two of Ben and Julia's children married. Their son Richard, who was well on the way to an impressive legal career, married Catherine Murray. Their daughter Mary married Captain Thomas Manners of the 49th British Regiment. Like her older sister Anne, Mary left the United States to live in Canada with her husband.

One night, several months after Jefferson's retirement from the presidency on March 4, 1809, Ben had a dream about his two old friends, Thomas Jefferson and John Adams. Although both men had helped shape the United States and both had served as president, now they were completely estranged from one another. In the years since they had signed the Declaration of Independence, Jefferson and Adams had come down on different sides of political debates and had lost their friendship. Ben, on the other hand, remained good friends with both men.

In his dream, Ben saw his son Richard holding a book. "What book is that in your hands?" he asked Richard.

"It is the history of the United States," Richard replied. "Shall I read a page of it to you?"

"No, no," Ben said. "I don't believe in the truth of any history except what is written in the Old and New Testaments."

"But, sir," Richard said, "this page relates to your friend Mr. Adams."

"Let me see it then," Ben said, taking the book. He read under the date 1809:

> Among the most extraordinary events of this year was the renewal of the friendship . . . between Mr. John Adams and Mr. Jefferson, the two ex-Presidents of the United States. . . . In the month of November 1809, Mr. Adams addressed a short letter to his friend Mr. Jefferson in which he congratulated him upon his escape to the shades of retirement and domestic happiness, and concluded it with assurances of his regard and good wishes for his welfare. This letter did great honor to Mr. Adams. It discovered a magnanimity known only to great minds. Mr. Jefferson replied to this letter and reciprocated expressions of regard and esteem.

Ben awoke from his dream, astonished at how clearly he recalled it. He also had a strong feeling he should somehow be involved in getting Adams and Jefferson back together. He wrote to Adams, telling him of the dream and urging him to write to Jefferson and congratulate him on his recent retirement. Adams did as Ben suggested, and Jefferson replied warmly. Ben was grateful his dream had come true. Two great men had been reconciled in their old age.

Ben and Julia's nine surviving children continued to grow and leave home. Everyone but John was doing well. In 1809 James graduated from the University of the State of Pennsylvania with a degree in medicine. In 1811 Ben was particularly proud when Richard was appointed Attorney General of Pennsylvania. The following year President James Madison named Richard Comptroller of the United States Treasury, and Richard moved to Washington, DC. At the same time, Ben's second to youngest son, Samuel, graduated from university and began studying law.

In 1812, at sixty-six years of age, Ben achieved one of the most important goals of his life. He published the book *Medical Inquiries and Observations upon the Diseases of the Mind.* It was the first psychiatric textbook published in the United States. Ben had spent most of his adult life pondering ideas of mental health and disease, and the book was a summary of what he had come to believe.

In the book, Ben argued that one of the main causes of insanity was diseased arteries in the brain that led to inflammation and poor circulation. He also argued that other causes included undernourishment, injury, poisons, overexposure to heat or cold, too much alcohol, tumors, abscesses, and exhausting labor. He pointed out that insanity could be inherited from one's parents or brought on by great shock, grief, or terror. Ben also observed that some people tended to be more prone to it than others. He had collected statistics that showed pregnant women and new mothers were at a higher risk for insanity, as were people who lived in cold, wet climates as opposed to those in warm, sunny ones.

Next Ben went to great lengths outlining ideas he had come across in his efforts to find cures for insanity. He noted that Dr. John Lettsom, whom

Ben had met and spent time with in London, England, theorized that plunging affected people into hot and cold baths could be helpful. Ben conducted his own experiments but did not find the practice useful. He did, however, develop a chair to restrain his patients who were agitated or experiencing "morbid excitement." This chair, known as the tranquilizer, was a large, wooden armchair. The patient sat in it—or was held down in it—and a large clamp was brought down over his or her head to lock it in place. The patient's arms and legs were strapped down too, immobilizing the body.

Another device that Ben invented was a gyrator. This invention was a large turntable upon which a patient was strapped. The turntable was turned rapidly for the opposite effect: instead of calming patients, it agitated them. However, Ben soon discovered that this normally made patients behave even more erratically.

Ben was interested in trying anything that would help patients. This was partly because his oldest son, John, was now a long-term patient in the insane ward at Philadelphia Hospital. John had always been difficult, but in the early 1800s he had started to drink heavily and became involved in a duel after a misunderstanding with a friend. In the duel he had shot and killed his friend. Although it was not illegal to kill someone in a mutually agreed-upon duel, losing his friend played heavily on John's mind. He stopped combing his hair or washing himself. In 1810, he had a mental breakdown and returned to his parents' home. But Ben could do nothing with him. John locked himself in a room and refused to talk. Finally, Ben had him admitted to the hospital, where he remained.

Ben read about a New York doctor who treated a woman for drug addiction by offering her snuff from a large snuff box. When the patient opened the box, a snake slithered out and onto her shoulder instead. According to the doctor, the shock of seeing the snake cured the woman's addiction. Ben tried this "shock" treatment out on his patients. He even tried using electricity to shock them out of their problems.

On January 4, 1813, Ben turned sixty-seven. Although he was a grandfather six times over, he still worked hard. He had patients to visit and lectures to plan. However, on Wednesday, April 14, Ben was sitting down to dinner with Julia and their youngest child, eleven-year-old William, when he began feeling ill and retired to his bedroom. That night he developed a fever and severe pains in his side. The following day several doctor friends visited. Most of them thought Ben had typhus, but Ben was sure it was tuberculous of the lungs. Either way, little could be done for him.

Ben called his family to his side, and over Easter weekend those who lived nearby came to say goodbye. On Monday, April 19, 1813, Ben spoke his last words to his son, Dr. James Rush. "Be indulgent to the poor. God is the paymaster of the poor," he said. Soon afterward he died.

Ben was buried near his parents after a simple ceremony at Christ Church in Philadelphia. Many people—friends, doctors, scientists, politicians, rich and poor, black and white—attended his funeral. Together they represented the people for whom Benjamin Rush had tried to live a useful life.

Bibliography

Binger, Carl. *Revolutionary Doctor: Benjamin Rush (1746–1813)*. New York: Norton, 1966.

Brodsky, Alyn. *Benjamin Rush: Patriot and Physician*. New York: St. Martin's Press, 2004.

Douty, Esther Morris. *Patriot Doctor: The Story of Benjamin Rush*. New York: Julian Messner, 1959.

Hawke, David Freeman. *Benjamin Rush: Revolutionary Gadfly*. Indianapolis: Bobbs-Merrill, 1971.

Riedman, Sarah R., and Clarence C. Green. *Benjamin Rush: Physician, Patriot, Founding Father*. London: Abelard Schuman, 1964.

Rush, Benjamin. *The Autobiography of Benjamin Rush*. Princeton: Princeton University Press for the American Philosophical Society, 1948.

———. *The Selected Writings of Benjamin Rush*, edited by Dagobert D. Runes. New York: Philosophical Library, 1947.

About the Authors

Janet and Geoff Benge are a husband and wife writing team with more than thirty years of writing experience. Janet is a former elementary school teacher. Geoff holds a degree in history. Together they have a passion to make history come alive for a new generation of readers.

Originally from New Zealand, the Benges make their home in the Orlando, Florida, area.

Heroes of History are available in paperback, e-book, and audiobook formats, with more coming soon! Unit Study Curriculum Guides are available for many biographies.

www.EmeraldBooks.com

Also from Janet and Geoff Benge...

More adventure-filled biographies for ages 10 to 100!

Christian Heroes: Then & Now

Gladys Aylward: The Adventure of a Lifetime • 978-1-57658-019-6
Nate Saint: On a Wing and a Prayer • 978-1-57658-017-2
Hudson Taylor: Deep in the Heart of China • 978-1-57658-016-5
Amy Carmichael: Rescuer of Precious Gems • 978-1-57658-018-9
Eric Liddell: Something Greater Than Gold • 978-1-57658-137-7
Corrie ten Boom: Keeper of the Angels' Den • 978-1-57658-136-0
William Carey: Obliged to Go • 978-1-57658-147-6
George Müller: Guardian of Bristol's Orphans • 978-1-57658-145-2
Jim Elliot: One Great Purpose • 978-1-57658-146-9
Mary Slessor: Forward into Calabar • 978-1-57658-148-3
David Livingstone: Africa's Trailblazer • 978-1-57658-153-7
Betty Greene: Wings to Serve • 978-1-57658-152-0
Adoniram Judson: Bound for Burma • 978-1-57658-161-2
Cameron Townsend: Good News in Every Language • 978-1-57658-164-3
Jonathan Goforth: An Open Door in China • 978-1-57658-174-2
Lottie Moon: Giving Her All for China • 978-1-57658-188-9
John Williams: Messenger of Peace • 978-1-57658-256-5
William Booth: Soup, Soap, and Salvation • 978-1-57658-258-9
Rowland Bingham: Into Africa's Interior • 978-1-57658-282-4
Ida Scudder: Healing Bodies, Touching Hearts • 978-1-57658-285-5
Wilfred Grenfell: Fisher of Men • 978-1-57658-292-3
Lillian Trasher: The Greatest Wonder in Egypt • 978-1-57658-305-0
Loren Cunningham: Into All the World • 978-1-57658-199-5
Florence Young: Mission Accomplished • 978-1-57658-313-5
Sundar Singh: Footprints Over the Mountains • 978-1-57658-318-0
C. T. Studd: No Retreat • 978-1-57658-288-6
Rachel Saint: A Star in the Jungle • 978-1-57658-337-1
Brother Andrew: God's Secret Agent • 978-1-57658-355-5
Clarence Jones: Mr. Radio • 978-1-57658-343-2
Count Zinzendorf: Firstfruit • 978-1-57658-262-6
John Wesley: The World His Parish • 978-1-57658-382-1
C. S. Lewis: Master Storyteller • 978-1-57658-385-2

David Bussau: Facing the World Head-on • *978-1-57658-415-6*
Jacob DeShazer: Forgive Your Enemies • *978-1-57658-475-0*
Isobel Kuhn: On the Roof of the World • *978-1-57658-497-2*
Elisabeth Elliot: Joyful Surrender • *978-1-57658-513-9*
Paul Brand: Helping Hands • *978-1-57658-536-8*
D. L. Moody: Bringing Souls to Christ • *978-1-57658-552-8*
Dietrich Bonhoeffer: In the Midst of Wickedness • *978-1-57658-713-3*
Francis Asbury: Circuit Rider • *978-1-57658-737-9*
Samuel Zwemer: The Burden of Arabia • *978-1-57658-738-6*
Klaus-Dieter John: Hope in the Land of the Incas • *978-1-57658-826-2*
Mildred Cable: Through the Jade Gate • *978-157658-886-4*
John Flynn: Into the Never Never • *978-1-57658-898-7*
Charles Mulli: We Are Family • *978-1-57658-894-9*
Richard Wurmbrand: Love Your Enemies • *978-1-57658-987-8*
John Newton: Change of Heart • *978-1-57658-909-0*

Available in paperback, e-book, and audiobook formats.
Unit Study Curriculum Guides are available for many biographies.
www.ywampublishing.com